Contents

CW01501999

Employee Engagement and Wellbeing Explained

Employee Engagement and Wellbeing Explained

Gemma Dale

KoganPage

First published in Great Britain and the United States in 2025 by Kogan Page Limited

Kogan Page
Kogan Page Ltd, 2nd Floor, 45 Gee Street, London EC1V 3RS, United Kingdom
Kogan Page Inc, 8 W 38th Street, Suite 902, New York, NY 10018, USA
www.koganpage.com

EU Representative (GPSR)
Authorised Rep Compliance Ltd, Ground Floor, 71 Baggot Street Lower, Dublin D02 P593, Ireland
www.arccompliance.com

Kogan Page books are printed on paper from sustainable forests.

ISBNs
Hardback   978 1 3986 2449 8
Paperback   978 1 3986 2450 4
Ebook   978 1 3986 2451 1

British Library Cataloguing-in-Publication Data
A CIP record for this book is available from the British Library.

Typeset by Hong Kong FIVE Workshop, Hong Kong
Printed and bound by CPI Group (UK) Ltd, Croydon CR0 4YY

Introduction

Introducing this book

This book has been written with the early-career Human Resources (HR) professional in mind. You may be undertaking your first role in HR or be in the early stages of your HR career. People managers may also find this book helpful if they want to build their skills in engaging their teams and supporting their wellbeing.

The book aims to provide both evidence and research on the two important topics of employee engagement and employee wellbeing, while also providing practical advice and guidance on how you can influence them within your organization. Understanding the research and theories on these topics can help you, as an HR professional, to offer sound, evidence-based advice to your organization and its managers. In turn, this will help to build your practical skills, and your credibility as a trusted partner.

Depending on your HR role, you may or may not currently be involved in delivering each of the areas addressed in this book. However, we have aimed to provide a comprehensive summary of each topic and how it is practically implemented in organizations so that you can gain a full understanding.

Throughout the book, you will find a range of reflection points, tips and exercises. Each of the tips is based on recognized good practice for engagement and wellbeing. Many chapters include 'What would you do?' exercises, which encourage you to think through how you could act in scenarios you are likely to encounter in your role. Suggested responses to these exercises are given at the end of this book. Each chapter also has review questions to test your learning and understanding, as well as further reading suggestions. Use the endnotes to find out more about the research that's discussed throughout. Remember that new research and insights are always being generated, so keeping up to date is important, too.

The reflection points, review questions and exercises included throughout the chapters are designed to deepen your learning and set the subjects of engagement and wellbeing in your unique organizational context. Not every exercise will necessarily be relevant to your current role and responsibilities; you should undertake the ones that you feel are most relevant to you and your role or the direction you wish to pursue in your future career. Remember that the HR role is a broad one, and you should consider any tips and suggestions in the context of your organizational culture. Depending on where you are based, there may also be local laws that relate to some of the subjects in this book, especially in relation to health and wellbeing, so before making recommendations or taking action, always check if there are any additional requirements you should consider.

If you are not currently in an HR role but aspire to be, there is plenty for you in this book, too. When you come to a reflection exercise or activity, you can think about this from a hypothetical perspective or think about jobs that you have had in the past, even if they have not been in HR.

The Conclusion provides further guidance on how you can assess your current skills, as well as some top tips and recommendations for action, all helping you to continue to learn about employee engagement and wellbeing.

An overview of employee engagement and wellbeing

Employee engagement and wellbeing are of considerable interest to many organizations. Healthy, happy employees are believed to be more productive, more committed and less likely to leave or take sickness absence from work. There are clear benefits for the organization of having engaged and motivated employees, as it contributes to the bottom line. Employees who are unhealthy or unhappy may be more likely to leave their jobs, have lower levels of performance and productivity, or take more absences. Each of these can lead to increased costs for the organization. The topics of employee engagement and wellbeing overlap. Research suggests that organizations that work on both engagement and wellbeing concurrently see more positive results than those that address the two areas separately.[1]

What is good for employee engagement is also often good for employee wellbeing. Some of what we know helps employees to feel engaged with their work and their employer can also enable them to be healthy. Similarly, some of those factors that we know are damaging to employee engagement or motivation can also be a cause of stress or poor health. It is, therefore, helpful to consider these subjects holistically. When we improve one element, we may also, in turn, improve the other. When we work at improving them both, there can be many mutual benefits for both organizations and the people that work for them.

The structure of this book

The first four chapters in this book consider employee engagement. Chapter 1 introduces the topic, discussing just what we mean by the term, why it matters to organizations, the difficulty with achieving and maintaining employee engagement, and HR's role in it. Chapter 2 focuses on the evidence for employee engagement, considering what might drive or enable engagement to thrive. Chapter 3 explores how organizations measure and understand how engaged employees feel, discussing the various mechanisms that can be used to achieve this understanding. Chapter 4 discusses how organizations and HR professionals can seek to improve employee engagement and the practical activities, events and initiatives that can support this aim.

The book then turns to our second subject: employee health and wellbeing. Chapter 5 introduces wellbeing, looking at the different definitions and terms that are in use and discussing what can support or detract from employee health and wellbeing in organizations. In Chapter 6, we deep dive into wellbeing interventions, considering what organizations do in practice to support employee engagement and reviewing what we know about the evidence for and against these different approaches.

Chapters 7 and 8 consider engagement and wellbeing together. Chapter 7 looks more closely at how you can support engagement and wellbeing in your organization through the work that you do, including practical activities and initiatives. Chapter 8 takes a similar approach, but from a manager's perspective. How do they influence engagement and how can HR professionals help them in this aspect of their role?

Finally, the Conclusion provides the opportunity to reflect on your current skills, behaviours and knowledge and plan for future learning and development. It also considers some of the challenges that are unique to the work of HR, and how these can be overcome.

Endnote

1 https://www.cipd.org/globalassets/media/knowledge/knowledge-hub/reports/full-report18364.pdf

CHAPTER ONE

Introducing engagement

Introduction

In the Introduction, we discussed the importance of employee engagement to organizations, highlighting how engaged employees contribute to business outcomes and the challenges that can arise from having disengaged employees. This chapter considers employee engagement in more depth. We define what we mean by employee engagement and consider whether people's understanding of the term is always consistent. This discussion is accompanied by a handy guide to related terms that can be used alongside engagement. We explore the different ways people and researchers think about engagement and look at the available data on how engaged employees are globally – as well as some potential problems with engagement.

Finally, we introduce the role of HR professionals in employee engagement, a subject that we will return to for a more in-depth review later in the book.

LEARNING OBJECTIVES

By the end of this chapter, you will be able to:

• Define employee engagement and provide a brief history of the term.

• Explain the importance of employee engagement.

• Articulate why engagement is problematic for many organizations.

• Describe what makes employees engaged at work and what can disengage them.

• Demonstrate how people can sometimes become too engaged with their work.

• Explain HR's role in employee engagement.

What is employee engagement?

Employee engagement: A broad term that encompasses how employees feel about their work and their employer, including their level of commitment, motivation and job satisfaction.

Employee engagement is a term first used in the early 1990s and is attributed to the organizational psychologist William Kahn, based at Boston University's Questrom School of Business.[1] For Kahn, employee engagement is how employees 'express themselves physically, cognitively, and emotionally' while at work. The term is often used to describe how an employee feels about their work or the organization they work for – it is a psychological state. The Institute of Employment Studies based in the UK has a different definition, calling engagement 'a positive attitude held by the employee towards the organization and its values'.[2]

Employee engagement is often linked with other ideas such as job satisfaction, motivation, commitment to work and effort. It's also often associated with employees who 'go the extra mile' or give discretionary effort to their work. It can include the extent to which employees identify with their work or the meaning they find in it. As you can already see, the term means different things to different people.

The theory underpinning the idea of employee engagement is a straightforward one. If employees are engaged, it is believed that they will do better work or be more productive, which, in turn, results in positive outcomes both for them as individuals and for the employer. This idea naturally makes the concept of considerable interest to employers. If they ensure their employees are engaged, they can gain the associated benefits. However, evidence from a range of sources does seem to suggest that many employees globally are not actually very engaged at work at all – and, in fact, many are actively disengaged (or unhappy) at work.

Defining employee engagement

Although the term 'employee engagement' is in common use, there is no single agreed-upon definition. We have already considered Kahn's definition of engagement, which focuses on how employees behave at work and how they feel. He saw engagement as something that might ebb and flow over time. His research identified that there are three important elements of engagement:

1 The psychological meaningfulness of work to the individual, derived from finding work worthwhile and valuable.
2 Safety, which is not about physical health and safety but instead a feeling that you can be your real self without fear of consequences. This is linked to feelings of trust, security, strong social systems and relationships within the workplace.

3 Psychological availability, which incorporates personal resources, physical and emotional energy, and having a sense of confidence in one's abilities.

An influential report into employee engagement called 'Engage for Success' by the voluntary movement of the same name, takes a slightly different view of engagement than the one provided by Khan.[3] Instead of seeing it as a feeling or an attitude or something an employee 'has', they see engagement as an 'organisational approach' – something that an organization does to ensure that their employees are committed and motivated to do their jobs, while also being able to have good wellbeing. This reframes engagement from Kahn's view, as something an employee has (or does not have), to something that an organization can do, usually through targeted activities, to make employees feel a certain way about their work.

Gallup, a global analytics and advisory organization that has measured employee engagement since 2009, has another perspective, describing employee engagement as the level of employee enthusiasm and involvement in their work and workplace.

The Chartered Institute of Personnel and Development (CIPD) in the UK describes employee engagement as an 'umbrella term' that covers a range of aspects of people management. Like Khan, they see engagement, as being a psychological state – a state of mind that employees experience, or what they think and feel about their work. They also recommend another way of looking at engagement, developed by psychologists at Utrecht University in the Netherlands.[4] This research (which uses the term 'work engagement' rather than 'employee engagement') suggests that engaged employees demonstrate three behaviours:

1 Vigour – the extent to which employees put effort or energy into their day-to-day work as well as persistence in the face of difficulties.

2 Dedication – employees' levels of enthusiasm and pride.
3 Absorption – the extent to which employees can become
  engrossed in their work so that time passes quickly.

Having so many ways of looking at employee engagement can
be challenging for HR professionals when trying to understand
how engaged our employees are and how we might influence
them to be more engaged. If we are not sure what it is or cannot
explain it well, it can be difficult to talk to managers and leaders
about it or build a business case for change. We will discuss
these challenges more in Chapter 2.

An important question that arises often in discussions about
employee engagement is: just what is it that employees are
engaged with? For example, are they engaged with their organization and its mission and purpose? Are they engaged with the
work that they do, regardless of the organization itself? Or is it
something else entirely? For example, think of a nurse. They
might be engaged with the purpose of their work, which is helping people or caring for them while they are unwell. They might
not, however, be engaged with their employer. They can also be
engaged but still find their work stressful. This complexity can
make it difficult to know how HR can influence employee
engagement. As this example suggests, there are many other
terms and concepts that overlap with employee engagement.

Related terms and concepts

As you read that last paragraph, you might have been thinking,
'Being engaged with the mission or purpose of your work sounds
like job satisfaction', or 'What's the difference between engagement and motivation?' Employee engagement is connected with
a range of elements in HR, many of which may be familiar to
you. We'll now discuss some of the related, and sometimes overlapping, terms and concepts.

JOB SATISFACTION

This term usually refers to how satisfied or content, overall, an individual is with their job. Just like with engagement, there are different definitions, but the one that is perhaps best known is from the psychologist Edwin Locke, from the University of Maryland, College Park, who describes it as our emotional state when we think about our jobs.[5] Although it is an overall assessment, it is usually considered to take into account different facets of the job, such as relationships with colleagues, the nature of the work and working conditions and opportunities to learn and grow. Locke says that job satisfaction is influenced by how closely what we want in a job, and what we have in a particular job, align. This suggests that while organizations and managers can influence job satisfaction, some of our feelings on satisfaction will depend on our personal values and desires – which are potentially outside of the control of the employer.

MOTIVATION

Motivation is a term that has multiple definitions. Generally, it is considered to be an internal state – a feeling or need that drives a particular behaviour. It can also be thought of as our desire to do something. In a workplace context, motivation incorporates an employee's feelings towards their work. It might include their desire to achieve objectives, earn money, progress or simply do a good job. Motivation can be separated into two forms: extrinsic motivation and intrinsic motivation. When we are extrinsically motivated, we have a desire to achieve an external goal, such as working towards a bonus or pay rise. Intrinsic motivation refers to a desire to do something because it is interesting or satisfying.

PSYCHOLOGICAL CONTRACT

This term is used to describe the unwritten agreement between an employee and their employer, comprised of the employee's beliefs and expectations about their job and their work. A fairly nebulous idea, it includes expectations about how they will be treated, what the working relationship will be like in practice and what commitments are made to each other – but these are not necessarily the same commitments as those written down in a contract of employment. For example, the contract of employment will state the amount of pay an employee is to receive, but the psychological contract might include the belief that the pay will be fair, or that pay decisions will be reasonable ones. These ideas may change over time, and expectations may differ. This idea is linked to employee engagement and levels of motivation. If an employee feels that their psychological contract has been breached, this may show up in their engagement or how they behave in the workplace.

EMPLOYEE EXPERIENCE

Employee experience is another concept related to employee engagement, and there is some crossover between engagement and the employee lifecycle (a topic we discuss in Chapter 7). Employee experience is a general term that is used to describe the total experience an employee has of working for a particular employer. It includes HR activities such as induction or training, but is much broader than that, encompassing the systems employees use, the interactions that they have with people who work for the organization, the workplace itself and ways of working. A good overall experience can help to support employee engagement. This idea is gaining increasing interest, and some organizations are now thinking about how to design for a good employee experience as well as aim to improve employee engagement.

DISCRETIONARY EFFORT

Discretionary effort refers to the level of effort employees voluntarily choose to apply at work, beyond the minimum required to fulfil their responsibilities. It may take the form of extra energy, extra time – or even enthusiasm. The concept of discretionary effort has come in for criticism; some people think it is wrong to ask employees to give more than is necessary to get their job done. Unintended consequences of too much discretionary effort may be stress, burnout or conflict between work and non-work aspects of life.

ORGANIZATIONAL COMMITMENT
This concept typically refers to an employee's loyalty or attachment to their organization, incorporating their intentions to stay or leave.

As you can see, there is some crossover between these different ideas and concepts, many of which you may have already studied as part of your wider HR learning. It can be difficult to articulate just how these concepts differ from employee engagement.

The CIPD believes that employee engagement goes further than the somewhat narrower ideas of motivation and satisfaction, looking at the employee experience and feelings about work more broadly. This is a useful frame of reference to understand how your employee engagement work might fit in with different elements of your HR role.

KEY POINTS

The CIPD suggests that, to address the challenges of defining employee engagement, HR professionals might find it useful to explain what they mean when talking to others about the subject. For example, 'When I talk about employee engagement, I mean…'. Be clear if you are using it as an umbrella term to describe a range of different elements of good people management and theories.

We will now go on to explore just why engagement is important for organizations.

Why engagement matters

There has been a great deal of research undertaken into employee engagement. Some of this is academic research published in journals. There is also a wide range of information and research published by consultancies specializing in working with organizations to understand and improve their employee engagement. This research has identified a range of reasons why organizations should focus on ensuring their employees are engaged, including financial and non-financial benefits that result from an engaged workforce.

Evidence suggests that engaged employees perform better and are more likely to go 'above and beyond'.[6] Engage for Success's report, which we discussed earlier in this chapter, found that engagement can impact positively on employee absence, retention, productivity, innovation and customer service.[7] All of these are desirable outcomes for an organization. Other studies have identified that engaged employees are less likely to change jobs, are more likely to be positive about their organization to others and are more receptive to organizational change. When employees are not engaged, they may be more likely to quit, withdraw any discretionary effort, take more absences or just simply be demotivated and less productive.

It is not just organizations that benefit from high engagement – employees do too. When employees are engaged and enjoying their work, they tend to feel empowered and have good psychological wellbeing.[8] Customers of organizations with engaged employees typically receive better service and, in turn, become more loyal.

In Chapter 2, we consider some debates about the viability of the evidence base for employee engagement. These debates do not mean that employee engagement isn't important, but they do mean that HR professionals should be mindful about not overstating what it can deliver for the organization. In Chapter 4, we look at how organizations can increase employee engagement. Many of the actions or initiatives we discuss not only support engagement but also support a strong organizational culture that will make somewhere a good place to work. Another challenge for employee engagement is the extent to which organizations can influence (or increase) it. Some of the factors that influence engagement, discussed in more depth in Chapter 2, are within the control of the organization and its managers, but some are not.

The evidence suggests that when approached effectively, taking into account the research (and its limitations – see Chapter 2) and balancing this with a thoughtful understanding of their workforce and unique context, organizations can benefit from taking a strategic approach to employee engagement. But there's a problem. Despite the increased interest in employee engagement over the last several decades, many employees are not engaged.

The engagement problem

> **Disengagement:** Mentally withdrawing from work, often as a result of dissatisfaction.

Gallup regularly publishes data on the state of engagement. Although they have found that engagement has steadily risen during the years they have been tracking it, in 2024 they still found that only 23 per cent of employees globally are engaged. Fifteen per cent are actively disengaged (we will consider what we mean by this later), and 62 per cent are not engaged.[9] Gallup argues that this lack of engagement comes with a significant cost to the global economy. CIPD data backs this up. It has also found that many employees are not engaged and has reported on employees feeling excessive pressure, uninspired by their organization's purpose and lacking in energy. This data hasn't changed significantly for five years.[10] It suggests that there is the potential to improve engagement in many organizations, which is a joint responsibility between leaders, people managers and HR professionals.

The term 'quiet quitting' is sometimes used to describe employees who are not engaged. They go to work but fulfil only the basic responsibilities of their roles, completing the work that is required of them but avoiding any extra effort, additional tasks or discretionary effort. They might just do the minimum that they can get away with. These employees have mentally 'checked out' of their jobs or organizations; they are not especially motivated, engaged or enthusiastic. Some employees who are 'quiet quitting' are looking for another role, taking the approach because they are unhappy more broadly with their job or employer. Others may not be looking to leave but are simply not willing to go above and beyond.

What engages and disengages employees?

There are many reasons why employees feel disengaged. It may be related to pay or terms and conditions, the work itself, their relationship with colleagues or managers, workload or lack of opportunities for development or progression. Disengagement can also be related to organizational culture. Even if an employee likes their day-to-day job, if they work in an unpleasant environment, or where there are cultural issues such as favouritism, blame or conflict, it may be difficult to feel positive about work.

Just like with engagement, there are different ideas about what 'disengagement' means. Sometimes, a distinction is made between employees who are not engaged and who are actively disengaged. The former might simply be neutral and not trying very hard (such as the quiet quitter). The latter, on the other hand, might be so unhappy or dissatisfied that it negatively affects their behaviour and, by extension, those who have to work with them.

> **STOP AND THINK**
>
> Do you think disengagement is necessarily a bad thing? Can you be disengaged from your job (or an aspect of it) and still do it well?

One study by Ashridge Education Centre in the UK went even further, categorizing employees into four zones of engagement: contentment, engaged, disengaged and pseudo-engaged.[11] For them, employees are disengaged when people feel unappreciated, there are low levels of trust within teams and the organizational culture is unhealthy. They suggest that employees who are pseudo-engaged work together reasonably enough but don't seek to help each other. For the pseudo-engaged, relationships are weak, and individuals are keen to say and do the 'right things' to get ahead.

> **EXERCISE**
>
> Ashridge Education Centre's research into engaged employees and teams suggests that they have some of the following attributes:
>
> - Teams work together to solve problems.
> - Diversity.
> - There is a positive atmosphere.
> - People feel empowered and valued.
> - There is a shared belief the team can achieve together.
> - People can respectfully disagree.
>
> Reflect on your organization or the team that you work in. Can you identify any of those attributes? Do you agree that these are hallmarks of engaged teams and employees? Is there anything else that you would add to this list based on your experiences?

Who is engaged?

Research suggests that demographic differences can influence who is engaged – and who is not. For example, the more education someone has, the more likely they are to be engaged, and employees who have permanent contracts are, perhaps unsurprisingly, more engaged than those who don't.[12] The same research identified that industry and occupation are also highly relevant to engagement levels; managers and people in professional knowledge work are typically more engaged than those who undertake manual or support occupations.

The CIPD made similar findings in their Good Work Index, identifying that those with higher levels of pay and seniority, as well as higher levels of qualification, are generally more engaged.[13] They also found that voluntary sector workers were more engaged than non-voluntary sector workers.

However, the expectation that everyone could or should be engaged is a high one, and is potentially unrealistic. Some work is dangerous, difficult, or physically and emotionally demanding. Other work is routine, repetitive or boring. Jobs can take people away from their families and require them to work long hours or with difficult people. In such cases, even if there are positive or enjoyable elements of a job, it might be difficult to maintain a positive attitude, or the vigour and absorption called for by some definitions of engagement.

When we consider global employee engagement, we cannot overlook the fact that some employees are undertaking their jobs in unpleasant or even dangerous working environments. Others undertake their work in countries with few employment protections, where employees have little power or job security. Engagement as a concept, in such circumstances, may be problematic.

Even when work is purposeful and meaningful to the person undertaking it, and when many of the conditions for employee engagement are present, it might still occasionally be stressful or draining. Consider, for example, someone who works in the emergency services. They might find their work meaningful, be content with their working conditions and have a great manager. At the same time, their job might involve dealing with extremely difficult or distressing situations. Their feelings towards their work and their organization might, therefore, fluctuate.

STOP AND THINK

Apply the ideas in this chapter to your current role, if you have one. List:

1 Elements of your role that you find engaging.

2 Elements that you do not find engaging.

Do they align with the theories discussed here?

Consider your role, manager, organization and your motivations and values in your answer.

The dark side of employee engagement

Employee engagement is generally presented as something desirable, especially for organizations and managers. Having enjoyable, interesting and absorbing work is, of course, also good for those who undertake it.

There can, however, be a darker side to employee engagement. Some employees can be too engaged. Research has identified that those who are highly engaged in their work can find it hard to switch off and, therefore, work excessive hours. Although this is typically voluntary and results from enthusiasm and enjoyment in their work, such working patterns can still be bad for health and wellbeing and can even result in burnout. Consider a teacher who worries about their students when they are not at school, or a leader who feels compelled to constantly check work devices. They may appear engaged when we compare their enthusiasm or commitment to typical definitions of employee engagement, but in practice, they may be experiencing negative personal outcomes from their engagement levels. HR professionals should bear this in mind when seeking to improve employee engagement, especially if they work in industries where this might be a particular risk.

> **TIP**
>
> With the rise of working from home, as well as many people now having work emails or messages on their phones, it is easy for those who are very invested in their jobs to overwork. Employees may benefit from policies about switching off or digital wellbeing.

HR and employee engagement

HR professionals' work on employee engagement typically falls into one of two areas:

1 Understanding and measuring engagement.
2 Seeking to improve engagement.

We will discuss these two areas briefly, returning to them later in the book for more detailed consideration.

Understanding and measuring engagement

This area of work focuses on understanding how employees feel about their work and organization. It includes a range of approaches, from broad surveys that seek to identify an overall view of engagement at an organization-wide level to more focused efforts to understand employee perceptions and attitudes. HR professionals often manage these different ways of getting feedback, disseminating results and supporting subsequent action planning. We cover this more in Chapter 3.

Improving engagement

Organizations often wish to improve employee engagement and will undertake a range of different activities to do so. HR professionals often manage these activities or initiatives in partnership with leaders and managers. They can include leadership and management development, events, employee benefits provision or employee voice activities. We cover this more in Chapter 4.

Employee voice: All the activities through which employees provide feedback, share ideas and communicate perspectives or concerns to their employer.

CHAPTER SUMMARY

- There are many different definitions of employee engagement, some from academia and some from organizations that research and promote the concept.

- Several other terms and theories relate to employee engagement, including motivation theories, job satisfaction and the employee experience.

- Research suggests that engaged employees are good for business, contributing to business outcomes such as improved customer service and productivity.

- Not everyone is engaged; it is estimated that less than a quarter of employees globally feel engaged with their work.

- HR professionals are typically involved in activities relating to understanding and measuring engagement and seeking to improve it.

REVIEW QUESTIONS

1 Write your own definition of employee engagement, based on this chapter.

2 Explain why organizations should focus on employee engagement.

3 Name three benefits of an engaged workforce.

Further reading

Bridger, E (2022) *Employee Engagement: A practical introduction*, 3rd ed, Kogan Page

MacLeod, D and Clarke, N (2009) Engaging for success: Enhancing performance through employee engagement, BIS, https://engageforsuccess.org/wp-content/uploads/2021/02/Engaging-for-Success.pdf (archived at https://perma.cc/4KZL-DAFE)

Endnotes

1 Kahn, W A (1990) Psychological conditions of personal engagement and disengagement at work, *Academy of Management Journal*, 33(4), pp 692–724

2 www.employment-studies.co.uk/report-summaries/report-summary-drivers-employee-engagement (archived at https://perma.cc/Y2U3-2B8R)

3 https://engageforsuccess.org/wp-content/uploads/2021/02/Engaging-for-Success.pdf (archived at https://perma.cc/4KZL-DAFE)

4 www.wilmarschaufeli.nl/publications/Schaufeli/209.pdf (archived at https://perma.cc/N7HT-EXJG)

5 www.sciencedirect.com/science/article/abs/pii/0030507369900130 (archived at https://perma.cc/F2BE-TZRG)

6   https://onlinelibrary.wiley.com/doi/full/10.1111/ijmr.12077 (archived at https://perma.cc/PN2U-72HA)

7   https://engageforsuccess.org/nailing-the-evidence/ (archived at https://perma.cc/CYJ7-5WK2)

8   https://journals.sagepub.com/doi/full/10.1177/0972150916631082?c asa_token=9n62K6z1-CgAAAAA%3ADpCW3XWYfvxkIsruicJx4k RtTr6ALcSKwkH2GfVnFcsMjlS1PhYeB1oDgVVvsPiGzKp4qIubKdA3 (archived at https://perma.cc/5QH7-ACL5)

9   www.gallup.com/workplace/349484/state-of-the-global-workplace. aspx (archived at https://perma.cc/97VW-N729)

10   www.cipd.org/globalassets/media/knowledge/knowledge-hub/ reports/2024-pdfs/8625-good-work-index-2024-survey-report-1-web.pdf (archived at https://perma.cc/3683-S59B)

11   https://visit.hultef.com/research-shades-of-grey (archived at https://perma.cc/TR4B-7TS3)

12   https://dspace.library.uu.nl/bitstream/handle/1874/389753/ application_pdf_2_.pdf?sequence=1 (archived at https://perma.cc/ GF3U-GCCD)

13   www.cipd.org/uk/knowledge/reports/goodwork/ (archived at https://perma.cc/R3GE-6R2S)

CHAPTER TWO

Evidence for engagement

Introduction

As we have already seen in Chapter 1, there are different viewpoints about what employee engagement is, how to achieve it, and the engagement challenge. We also discussed how employee engagement overlaps with other, related ideas about work.

This chapter considers the evidence base for engagement. It provides an overview of relevant theories and research into employee engagement and what might be enablers and drivers of engagement at work. We also consider some criticisms of employee engagement as a concept, including challenges about the evidence. Finally, we look at academic theories relating to employee engagement.

These discussions will help you to build your knowledge about this important HR topic. Being able to demonstrate your understanding of the related issues, including the challenges, will help you to be seen as a trusted and credible professional. In turn, this knowledge will help you to respond to questions and challenges from within your organization, contribute to the development of business cases and ensure that your resources are used in the best possible way.

LEARNING OBJECTIVES

By the end of this chapter, you will be able to:

- Explain the main drivers and enablers of employee engagement.

- Identify potential criticisms and challenges relating to employee engagement and how these can be addressed within your organization.

- Demonstrate the importance of evidence-based decision-making as an HR professional.

- Summarize key academic theories that relate to employee engagement.

Drivers of engagement

To improve levels of engagement, a topic that we will return to in detail later, we first need to understand what causes or drives engagement.

Research undertaken by Engage for Success, an organization in the UK promoting employee engagement, determined four broad drivers of engagement within organizations, which they refer to as 'enablers':

- A strategic narrative, set by leaders, which explains the organization's purpose and direction.
- Engaging managers who treat their people as individuals, giving them scope, and stretching and coaching them so they can reach their full potential.
- A focus on employee voice with plenty of opportunities for employees to share feedback and be involved in decision-making.
- Organizational integrity – the organization has values that are embedded into the culture and are lived by leaders.[1]

Gallup, the engagement specialists, have a slightly different view. They argue that there are several drivers of employee engagement and enthusiasm:

- A caring manager.
- Deriving purpose and meaning from work.
- Development opportunities.
- Colleague relationships.
- Ongoing conversations.
- The ability to use and build on personal strengths in work.[2]

These different viewpoints highlight the difficulties in deciding just what we mean when we talk about what helps employees to feel engaged.

To help your understanding, we will now explore some of these potential drivers of engagement in more depth, as well as other influences on employee engagement.

Employee voice

As we have seen, employee voice has been said to be an enabler of employee engagement. This is a term used to describe ways in which employees get to have a say in their organizations. This can include everything from opportunities to provide feedback or make suggestions to formal communication mechanisms or annual employee surveys. Some organizations have formal 'listening strategies' where they have a plan for engaging with employees for feedback.

STOP AND THINK

- List the ways your organization currently encourages employee voice.
- What happens to the information that employees provide?
- Can you identify any other opportunities to increase employee voice?

Engaging managers

Managers have a key role to play in employee engagement due to their close working relationship with employees. They implement many of the activities that can influence engagement, including performance appraisals, recognition and learning and development opportunities. As we discuss in Chapter 8, developing people managers, especially in relation to their role in engagement, can help to improve overall engagement levels.

The MacLeod report into engagement found that engaging managers:

- coach and stretch their employees
- treat them as individuals
- make everyone feel part of the team
- provide clear objectives
- help team members understand how their work contributes to the objectives of the organization

Finally, they say that engaging managers are approachable, care about employees' welfare and provide praise and recognition.[3]

STOP AND THINK

Reflect on the following aspects of management in your organization:

- Do managers demonstrate behaviours that support employee engagement amongst their teams?

- Does the organization provide any tools, training or resources to help understand and improve employee engagement? List these.

- What resources or training could you, as an HR professional, advocate for or introduce to help managers become more skilled at enabling employee engagement?

Purpose

Purpose at work is linked to both engagement and motivation. A survey from global consultancy firm McKinsey found that around 70 per cent of people derive their purpose from their work.[4]

In his book *Drive*, Daniel Pink defines purpose as the sense of meaning that employees get from their work – a belief that the work is important or contributes to something bigger than us. Some research suggests that following the global pandemic, the desire for purpose and meaning at work increased, with employees thinking differently about the role of work in their lives.[5] Living through a complex situation, like a global health emergency, can encourage people to reflect on their lives and their futures.

Purpose is very personal. What gives one person a sense of purpose will not necessarily be true for another, even if they do the same work for the same company. Some people will also get their sense of purpose from the things they do outside of work. This can make it a challenging element of engagement, as it can be difficult to influence whether employees feel that their work has purpose or meaning, as purpose can link to our own values, beliefs or intrinsic motivations.

Strengths

Strengths are generally considered to be natural talents or abilities that an individual has. Employees can feel more engaged when they can use their strengths in their work and are allowed to develop them further. It is generally considered better to help employees identify their strengths and build upon them rather than try to tackle weaknesses. One survey by Gallup found that employees who can use their strengths at work are six times less likely to leave their jobs.[6] The use of strengths is also associated with employee wellbeing. Managers can play an important role in helping employees to identify and then improve their strengths.

Colleague relationships

Gallup survey employee engagement all over the world. One of the questions they ask is whether employees have a best friend at work. They believe that this is not only an important component in engagement but also influences people's intention to stay working for their employer. Having meaningful relationships and connections to others is a fundamental psychological need – as we shall explore later it is also related to health and wellbeing.

STOP AND THINK

Do you have a best friend at work? What do you think of this idea? Based on your own experiences of relationships at work, do you agree with Gallup that this is an important element of engagement?

Organizational values

In an organizational context, values are a set of stated principles or beliefs, set out by an organization. They typically reflect organizational culture and aim to say what the company stands for.

As individuals, we also have our own set of personal values – they are our beliefs about what matters in life (and in our work), and they can unconsciously guide our behaviour and priorities. When our personal values align with our organization's values, it can be a force for engagement.

Job design

Job design relates to the nature of the work itself, its roles, responsibilities and the way that tasks are undertaken, and it can influence employee engagement. Job design can also include demands, support and resources – in Chapter 3 we see how these can also influence engagement. Job design can include the speed at which people are required to work, the safety of the work that they do and the productivity that is required of the worker.

Job design can affect how interesting and fulfilling a job is and is linked to other ideas we have discussed in this section, including whether employees have opportunities to learn and grow and whether the work that they do is meaningful. When employees can determine how their work is done (a process sometimes known as 'job crafting'), it helps to support autonomy, which is good for motivation and engagement – as well as wellbeing.

Good leadership

While managers influence engagement through their day-to-day interactions with the people who work for them, senior leaders also influence engagement. Research has found that leaders who are seen as charismatic, ethical and authentic are all good for employee engagement.

Individual differences

So far, we have discussed the organizational factors that influence whether an employee is engaged. However, other non-work factors may affect employee engagement, too. The extent to which employees find meaning in work relates not just to the work itself but the personality, beliefs and values of the individual. We differ in many ways. We all have different levels of resilience, emotional intelligence, motivators, confidence and life experiences. These will naturally influence what engages us at work. For example, someone who values work-life balance might be engaged by an organization that prioritizes this and has associated HR policies.

Other factors that have been found to influence engagement include:

- working in a collaborative environment
- pay and reward, work-life balance
- diversity and inclusion
- career advancement opportunities
- pride in the organization
- HR practices and fairness of treatment

The role of pay and benefits in employee engagement

It is commonly assumed that pay is a motivator. In some circumstances, and for some individuals, this is true. However, financial reward is less important to some people than we might think. If people feel that pay is unfair, this might be a demotivator or cause of low engagement. Where there are opportunities to enhance pay, perhaps through bonuses or commissions, this might motivate or engage some employees, whereas others will be motivated by intrinsic factors instead.

EXERCISE

Reflect on the organizational drivers of employee engagement described in this section and consider your ways of working compared to them. Answer the following questions:

- Which of these drivers are present in your organization?
- Can you identify any gaps? For example, are there any drivers of employee engagement that seem to be underdeveloped or missing in your organization? These may be opportunities for improvement or recommendations.
- To what extent are the actions of managers and leaders aligned with the drivers of employee engagement?

Criticisms of employee engagement

As we have already seen, there are different perspectives about just what employee engagement is and how it can be achieved – as well as what outcomes may be derived from employee engagement. One common criticism of employee engagement is that the idea is nothing new. Critics point to much older research and theories that address similar ideas. They suggest that engagement is essentially therefore 'old wine in new bottles', presenting an idea of something new and important, which is simply a repackaging or relabelling (perhaps for commercial gain) of previous research and ideas.

The lack of a clear definition of employee engagement, as discussed in Chapter 1, is also highlighted as a problem. Academics have pointed out that this leads to confusion about what we are talking about, with the possibility that when we talk about it, we are all talking about a slightly different thing.[7] This, in turn, affects whether we can accurately measure engagement or understand whether any activity that we undertake in the name of engagement is having the desired outcome.

Finally, the evidence base for employee engagement is also subject to concern. There are several elements to this criticism:

- How can we effectively research a subject if we cannot agree on a definition? Where research suggests employee engagement is a good thing and will lead to positive outcomes, how can we be sure that this research is valid if we are potentially talking about different things?
- Some of the evidence about employee engagement is based on case studies from specific organizations that discuss how they have improved employee engagement and the benefits that they have experienced as a result. However, such case studies are likely to be influenced by their own circumstances, and what one organization has found will not necessarily be replicable in another, different situation.

We will explore what amounts to quality evidence later in this chapter, but as a general point there are very few in-depth studies of employee engagement at the higher levels of research quality.

TIP

Despite the potential issues with using case study evidence (as the outcomes in one organization cannot necessarily be replicated in another, different situation) they can be useful for generating new ideas and approaches. Looking externally to learn about the experiences of others can be a valuable source of insight. Examples can also be shared with leaders and managers. There is a range of case studies on employee engagement on the CIPD and Engage for Success websites.

Some studies into engagement are undertaken by organizations that have a vested interest in people taking employee engagement seriously and investing in it within their own organizations. Examples are management consultancy firms or the providers of engagement services. When it comes to the evidence for engagement, some have suggested that what we really have is evidence for correlation and not causation. This means that high levels of employee engagement do not necessarily directly cause positive business outcomes (such as high productivity). We cannot say this for certain. Neither can we say with certainty that investing in employee engagement will result in positive business outcomes. It may just be that the high engagement and the positive business outcomes are naturally occurring at the same time. Or perhaps it is the other way around – that the good business outcomes are driving employee engagement, because working for somewhere that is high performing feels good and engaging.

Why do these criticisms matter? Arguably, the aims of employee engagement are laudable ones. If we say that employee engagement is about making work and workplaces better, then it's a good thing. Do we need to pay attention to those who argue against it? We do. It is important for HR professionals to make evidence-based decisions and recommendations. Understanding these issues is important for credibility and will help to ensure that you do not make claims that you cannot substantiate.

TIP

It isn't unusual for HR professionals to receive pushback from managers in relation to key people topics, and employee engagement is no different. Managers can be time poor and are often focused on immediate operational pressures. They may view engagement efforts as time-consuming or adding to their to-do list. They may have had bad past experiences with HR initiatives, or generally fail to see the value of concepts like employee engagement.

So what can you do? Here are a few tips for dealing with critics of employee engagement. They apply to other HR topics too.

- Seek to understand their concerns or point of view. Ask questions and show a willingness to listen to their thoughts and perceptions.

- Equip yourself with relevant and quality evidence on the topic of engagement – but do not make claims that cannot be substantiated. Acknowledge limitations and do not 'over sell' the concept.

- Highlight how proposed engagement activities or initiatives align with their goals or can contribute to operational priorities.

- Demonstrate quick wins or share successes where engagement activities have previously delivered positive outcomes for the organization.

- Build your relationships. Good relationships will help you to engage managers with your suggestions and strategies.

Evidence-based decision making

The Centre for Evidence-Based Management, a non-profit organization based in The Netherlands, defines evidence-based decision-making as the process of making decisions using the best available evidence from multiple sources.[8] It involves thinking critically and analysing the evidence that we have. Sometimes we make decisions based on our own experiences (which will inevitably include bias and unconscious beliefs) or our own judgements and opinions. These are not necessarily the best sources of evidence, even when the person making that decision has plenty of experience. This isn't the only way that decisions are made in organizations. Often, ideas of so-called 'best practice' influence what organizations do, or decision-makers are influenced by what they have seen happen in other organizations. However, this ignores the importance of context – what works in one organization will not necessarily work in another. In evidence-based decision-making, the experiences, perspectives and ideas of managers and employees are still considered, but it is just one source of data that can be balanced against other sources.

Using quality evidence from a range of different sources helps to ensure that the decisions we make at work are robust, well-informed, and more likely to lead to successful outcomes tailored to the specific needs and context of the organization.

Note that while we are discussing evidence-based decision-making in our chapter on employee engagement, these principles also apply to our later discussions on actions and strategies for employee health and wellbeing.

EXAMPLE
Evidence-based decision making

After the Covid-19 pandemic, there was increased demand from employees for remote and hybrid work. Many employers allowed employees to work in a hybrid way – but others insisted their employees 'returned to office'. Often, office attendance mandates were accompanied by statements from leaders suggesting that office attendance was important for culture, innovation or team relationships. An evidence-based approach to deciding on office attendance policies would have considered the following:

- Academic research, published in reputable journals, into the impact of hybrid or remote work on issues like productivity, relationships and innovation – looking at both positive and negative effects.

- A review of internal data – an analysis of the organization's data (such as performance or productivity data, or HR records) into similar outcomes and effects.

- The experiences of other organizations that had allowed hybrid work or mandated a return to office policy, and an analysis of the views and opinions of different stakeholders.

These different sources of evidence can be aggregated and assessed to give a holistic view of the issue and inform decision-making.

Theories related to engagement and motivation

In Chapter 1, we identified that employee engagement is related to other concepts such as motivation, job satisfaction and the psychological contract. There is also a range of different academic theories that can help us think about and understand employee engagement. Some of these theories are also relevant to wellbeing, and we return to them later in the book. This section provides an overview of some of these theories. You will note that some of them have similar or overlapping ideas.

We briefly discussed motivation in Chapter 1. Many theories of motivation are related to ideas about employee engagement – some of these are about motivation in general, while others focus on work and the workplace. Motivational theories seek to understand and explain the underlying drivers of human behaviour, providing insights into why individuals act, persist or cease efforts toward certain goals. If we can understand what makes people behave the way that they do, we can design work accordingly to maximize motivation.

Maslow's hierarchy of needs

This is a framework that organizes human motivations into five levels and is often presented in the form of a triangle. Each level must be satisfied before the higher need becomes a motivating factor. At the base of the triangle are physiological needs like food and shelter, followed by safety needs for security and stability. Next are social needs, including love and belonging, and then esteem needs, such as recognition and self-respect. At the top of the triangle is self-actualization, where individuals strive to fulfil their potential and pursue personal growth.

Herzberg's two factor theory

This theory distinguishes between two sets of factors that influence employee motivation and satisfaction. The first set is known as hygiene factors and includes salary, job security and working conditions. These can prevent employees from becoming dissatisfied, but they do not actively motivate them. For example, you can pay people a salary that is high enough to prevent them from becoming demotivated by pay, but on its own, pay will not usually motivate anyone to work harder. In contrast, the other factors are motivators. These include achievement, recognition and opportunities for personal growth. They can drive satisfaction and employee performance. The theory suggests that addressing hygiene factors eliminates dissatisfaction, but true motivation requires emphasizing the motivating factors.

> **'Fit'**: A range of theories that consider the extent to which an individual and the work they do or their organization are a good fit for each other, or the extent to which an individual fits into a particular group or team at work. Fit theories can encompass a range of ideas, including whether an individual feels that they belong, or that their values align with those of their employers.

Job demands-resource

This theory is a well-known perspective that states that every job has its own unique set of demands and resources. As we will discuss later in our chapters on wellbeing, if a job has too many demands (or the individual also has too many personal demands) and these are not addressed, this can result in work-related stress or poor health outcomes. Demands might include high workloads, conflict or physical demands.

In contrast, if a job is plentiful in resources, such as good colleague relationships, opportunities to develop and learn or stimulating work, then this can be motivational and lead to increased work performance and engagement. This theory suggests that it is possible for organizations to design work and the workplace to maximize employee resources and reduce work demands.

Social exchange theory

This theory can be used to explain psychological processes, or how employees feel, in relation to their work. It states that relationships between employees and their employers are reciprocal. Therefore, if an employee feels that they are being treated well and that they work for a good employer, they will return this with effort and commitment – there is an exchange between them. This theory may help to explain how the process of engagement, and its possible beneficial outcomes, occurs in practice.

Job characteristics theory

This theory relates to the design of work, focusing on how to make work more interesting and satisfying. First developed in the 1970s, it recognizes that jobs that are routine and repetitive can lead to employee dissatisfaction or demotivation. The authors of the theory, Hackman and Oldman, identified five characteristics that, when applied to the design of a job, can lead to increased job satisfaction, motivation and employee performance:

1 Task significance – the meaning that the employee gains from doing the job.
2 Skill variety – the range of skills that the employee needs to undertake the job.
3 Feedback – the feedback provided to employees about their work performance.
4 Task identity – the extent to which an employee completes a task from start to finish or undertakes work with a visible outcome.
5 Autonomy – the amount of freedom and choice the employee has in determining how to do their job.[9]

When jobs are high in each of these core characteristics, positive outcomes should result for both the employee and the organization, such as high levels of performance, employee motivation and job satisfaction, and reduced turnover and employee absence. According to this theory, organizations should deliberately seek to maximize these characteristics in the design of work.

Self-determination theory

This motivation theory identifies that all people are driven by three basic needs:

1 The desire for autonomy.
2 The desire for competence.
3 The desire for relatedness (relationships with others).

In this theory, developed by Deci and Ryan, competency relates to a drive to grow and develop.[10] Relatedness refers to having a sense of belonging and attachment to other people. As well as identifying these basic needs, the theory goes on to set out how these needs can be either supported or thwarted by a particular context or situation. Applied to work, this means that a job or workplace can either support these needs, such as by helping people to grow and build meaningful relationships with others, or they can thwart them (by preventing them or failing to fulfil them). Supporting these needs will help to motivate employees, while thwarting them may result in the opposite effect. Just like the other theories discussed here, self-determination theory suggests that organizations can intentionally design work to maximize the potential for motivation and the additional benefits that this generates.

EXERCISE

Review the different academic theories summarized in this section, and the drivers of engagement that we discussed in Chapter 1. Make a list of any similarities you can identify.

WHAT WOULD YOU DO?
Number 1

A manager approaches you for advice on their team. They believe that the whole team is demotivated and lacks engagement. This has worsened in recent months, as the company has been under some financial pressure and, as a result, employees have been working longer hours. Some planned employee training and social events have also been cancelled and bonuses postponed.

Use the academic theories to consider what advice you would give to the manager in this scenario.

- Which theories would you draw on to explain the reduced motivation and engagement?

- Using the theories discussed in this section, can you make any recommendations for the manager to improve engagement and motivation?

CHAPTER SUMMARY

- Employee engagement can be influenced by numerous operational and personal factors, including organizational culture, management style, colleague relationships, leadership and the design of the work itself.
- Not everyone agrees with the evidence base for employee engagement. It is not a silver bullet solution for organizational challenges, and the idea has been subject to criticism.
- Understanding academic theories and other research related to engagement can help HR professionals provide good advice and evidence-based recommendations, enhancing their credibility.
- Theories and research can help to explain employee engagement, why employees may or may not feel engaged and how to increase engagement in our organizations.

REVIEW QUESTIONS

1 List three drivers or enablers of employee engagement.

2 What academic theories are related to ideas of employee engagement?

3 Why should HR professionals be informed by evidence when planning or undertaking employee engagement activities?

4 Identify ways that HR professionals can recognize signs of low engagement.

Further reading

CIPD (2021) Employee engagement: An evidence review, www.cipd.org/
uk/knowledge/evidence-reviews/evidence-engagement/ (archived at
https://perma.cc/3T4R-ZANT)

Barends, E and Rousseau, D (2018) *Evidence Based Decision Making: How
to use evidence to make better organizational decisions*, Kogan Page

Briner, R (2015) What is employee engagement and does it matter? An
evidence-based approach, https://engageforsuccess.org/wp-content/
uploads/2015/09/Rob-Briner.pdf (archived at https://perma.cc/
WG6K-8RJH)

Pink, D (2011) *Drive: The surprising truth about what motivates us*, Penguin

Endnotes

1 https://engageforsuccess.org/the-four-enablers/ (archived at https://
   perma.cc/383X-6NR3)

2 https://www.gallup.com/workplace/285674/improve-employee-
   engagement-workplace.aspx#ite-357473 (archived at https://perma.cc/
   EU4L-JLVJ)

3 https://engageforsuccess.org/wp-content/uploads/2021/02/Engaging-
   for-Success.pdf (archived at https://perma.cc/4KZL-DAFE)

4 https://www.mckinsey.com/capabilities/people-and-organizational-
   performance/our-insights/the-search-for-purpose-at-work (archived
   at https://perma.cc/35E7-Z2F4)

5 https://www.gartner.com/en/articles/employees-seek-personal-value-
   and-purpose-at-work-be-prepared-to-deliver (archived at
   https://perma.cc/7NLA-E427)

6 https://www.gallup.com/workplace/231605/employees-strengths-
   company-stronger.aspx (archived at https://perma.cc/79CC-N8MU)

7 https://engageforsuccess.org/wp-content/uploads/2015/09/Rob-
   Briner.pdf (archived at https://perma.cc/WG6K-8RJH)

8 https://cebma.org/resources/frequently-asked-questions/what-is-
   evidence-based-management/ (archived at https://perma.cc/DS82-QJVB)

9 Hackman, J R (1980) Work redesign and motivation, *Professional
   Psychology*, 11(3), 445–55

10 Deci, E L and Ryan, R M (1985) The general causality orientations
   scale: Self-determination in personality, *Journal of Research in
   Personality*, 19(2), 109–34

CHAPTER THREE

Measuring and understanding engagement

Introduction

Most organizations seek to increase engagement levels among their employees so that they can reap the benefits. To increase engagement, they must first understand their starting point. Measuring how employees currently feel about their work and the organization gives businesses the feedback they need to take action.

This chapter discusses the many different ways that organizations, and specifically HR professionals, can seek feedback from employees to assess engagement levels. We consider the benefits and drawbacks of each method and how to encourage employees to participate. The different methods are often referred to collectively as the 'employee voice'. We also look at ways that employee unhappiness (or disengagement) may show up in practice, as well as through these more formal approaches to measuring engagement.

Finally, we discuss the importance of acting upon feedback and developing action plans for change.

LEARNING OBJECTIVES

By the end of this chapter, you will be able to:

- Explain why organizations should seek to understand employee perspectives.

- Compare and evaluate different methods for understanding and measuring employee sentiment.

- Describe the challenges that come with measuring engagement.

- Articulate how to use employee surveys to measure engagement.

- Summarize how organizations can use engagement data to drive change.

The importance of employee perspectives

TIP

Before reading this chapter, identify the different ways that your organization seeks feedback from employees. This could include surveys, suggestions schemes, open meetings, trade union consultations or network groups. Then, check out the list of potential sources of feedback listed in this chapter – are there any that your organization does not currently utilize?

Information on the level of employee engagement can be invaluable for organizations and their leaders. It is data upon which decisions and improvements can be made. Identifying disengagement (and its potential sources) is equally important as it can allow an organization to address problem areas that might otherwise lead to retention issues or reduced motivation or productivity.

There is no single 'best' way to gather employee feedback, and organizations should tailor their approach based on their culture, resources and workforce dynamics, as well as practicalities. Whatever methods are chosen, they should encourage honest and constructive input. However, this is only likely if employees feel safe expressing their opinions openly and that their opinions will be genuinely heard and acted upon. Therefore, a key role for HR leaders and managers is to create an environment where employees are willing to speak up. Trust plays a foundational part in this – organizations with high-trust cultures will find that employees are more open and likely to participate in feedback. Listening and acting upon feedback creates a positive cycle of reinforcement, supporting and reinforcing that sense of trust.

In practical terms, HR departments are often the organization's owners of employee feedback mechanisms. They may be responsible for some or all of the following:

- Managing the processes of feedback.
- Identifying and managing relevant suppliers.
- Analysing and communicating the information shared by employees.
- Managing action planning for change.

HR professionals may also need to provide specialist advice to managers and leaders on appropriate ways to gather and act upon feedback, and sometimes gain buy-in for the process.

There are many reasons why learning about how employees think and feel about their work, manager and organization is a good idea. Whichever method you adopt to listen to employees or gain feedback, a formal, strategic approach to understanding employee perspectives can provide important insights into your people. Some people call this a listening strategy.

Listening strategy: An organization's formal plan for listening to employees, seeking feedback and gaining insights from them.

Employee feedback can lead to opportunities for improvement; employees are likely to have insights and ideas that may be valuable. Leaders do not necessarily have all the best ideas! Listening to employees can also help organizations to discover important issues or problems, perhaps before they escalate. Feedback can help leaders find out what they don't know. It can also allow organizations to track progress, either against goals or previous action plans.

Acting upon feedback can lead to an improved employee experience. In turn, this should lead to better engagement and reduced dissatisfaction and potential for demotivation. Overall, it can reduce employees' desire to quit.

Methods for understanding and measuring engagement

As we will discuss in the next section, the employee survey is one of the most common tools for seeking feedback and measuring levels of employee engagement. But it's not the only mechanism. The following sources of information can also provide useful data for organizations wanting to understand how their employees feel and gain their input into improvements:

- Existing sources of employee data, such as retention or exit interview data – this can provide information on what causes dissatisfaction to a level that makes someone want to leave the organization. Assessing any trend data on employee grievances may also indicate areas of concern and could point towards reasons why employees could become disengaged.

- Focus groups – these explore employee perceptions, perhaps from specific employee groups, or to take a detailed look at particular issues in the organization. These can be helpful to dive deeper into any areas that arise from a broader engagement survey.

- Stay interviews – these are informal conversations where organizations (usually through managers or HR) seek to understand an employee's motivation to stay with the organization.

- Pulse surveys – these surveys are often quite short and use a small number of regular questions so that important metrics can be tracked over time.

- Point-in-time surveys – these surveys are undertaken at a particular time in the employment lifecycle, for example, a new starter survey designed to assess the induction experience. They can provide insights into how well a particular process is working and whether it's contributing to engagement.

- Social media – sites like Glassdoor or Indeed allow employees (or job applicants) to rate your organization. There is often a focus on recruitment and the application experience. Comments are anonymous and, as such, cannot necessarily be verified, but these sites can be a useful source of data, especially if there are comments around similar themes.

- Suggestion schemes – a traditional mechanism, these are simply methods through which employees can make suggestions for improvement. While they don't necessarily tell you how people feel about their work, they can provide insights into what people may find frustrating or a barrier to working more effectively – potential sources of disengagement.

- Trade unions – engaging with trade unions (or other formal workplace consultation committees) can help organizations understand employee concerns and priorities. Feedback from trade unions can also provide a barometer for employee sentiment and provide an early warning system for any areas of collective concern that may negatively affect employee engagement.

There is no 'best' approach to seeking feedback from employees and assessing how they feel about their work, only the one that best fits the particular circumstances and provides the information that you need. Surveys allow for a range of questions and can reach all employees in a relatively short space of time. They might not provide a nuanced or in-depth picture, which can sometimes be gathered from processes like interviews or focus groups. These approaches can, however, take much more time and resources. If you need to recommend a way to find out information, consider the available options alongside practicalities such as time and resources. Pick the one(s) that are most likely to provide useful and meaningful information on which you will be able to act.

If you use a range of different methods to listen to employees, think about how you can integrate these different sources of information, presenting them to leaders and managers in an accessible way.

TIP

If you have different sources of employee feedback and perceptions, look for areas of similarity and difference when interpreting your data. These can be instructive. Similar feedback from different sources can suggest that the data has good validity, but differences can also provide insight. Consider what might be the reason for these differences.

Identifying disengagement

In Chapter 1, we briefly discussed the idea of disengagement. This broad term encompasses a range of negative employee feelings and perspectives. This might include putting in minimal effort or actively looking for other work. William Khan, who, as a reminder, first identified the concept of employee engagement, talks about disengagement as an act of withdrawing from work, either physically, cognitively or emotionally. Disengaged individuals remove their self and their energy from their work.

Many of the methods that can be used to assess levels of engagement will also be able to identify disengagement. Surveys (discussed in the next section) can include rating questions to identify quantitative measures that might indicate unhappiness, stress or quit intention.

TIP

Global consultancy firm McKinsey suggests that one way we can learn about disengagement levels is to ask employees whether they intend to look for another job in the next three to six months.[1]

WHAT WOULD YOU DO?
Number 2

It is sometimes said that you know employee engagement 'when you see it'. Assume that a manager comes to you and says they believe one of their employees is disengaged, which is affecting their work and the wider team.

• What questions would you ask the manager?

• How would you advise the manager to address the situation?

Think about the potential causes of disengagement when formulating your answer.

SPOTTING WARNING SIGNS

So far, we have discussed methods for assessing and understanding levels of employee engagement. There are, however, other ways to understand what is going on. Organizations are sometimes described as icebergs – what you see on the surface (and what people tell you about) is different from what's happening underneath (which is less well-known). Several potential warning signs could signify problems with levels of employee engagement or broader organizational culture. For example:

- High levels of sickness absence, especially for stress or repeated short-term absences.
- High employee turnover.
- A lack of willingness to provide feedback or participate in employee voice.
- Conflict, such as grievances or formal disputes.
- Low participation in activities or events.
- Evidence of blame or fear.
- Inappropriate employee behaviour.
- Damage to or lack of care for company property or facilities.
- Excessive working hours.

These examples do not necessarily indicate a problem, especially if they are occurring individually, but if they are recognized as regular occurrences, or several of them are apparent at any one time, this may warrant reflection or investigation.

The challenges with measuring engagement

There are several challenges when it comes to measuring engagement. The first of these relates to the definition issue we discussed in Chapter 1. What are we *actually* seeking to measure? For example, is it how much people like their work or their employer, how likely they are to leave, or how motivated they are? These are all different things, and it is important before seeking any feedback to be clear about what it is you want to know, and then check that your chosen method for employee feedback is going to properly answer your questions.

As not every employee will take part in a survey or any other method for providing feedback, it is always difficult to be sure that you are getting a truly representative sample of views. It may be that those employees who are most unhappy and want to highlight their concerns are more likely to provide feedback. It could also be argued that those who are most engaged don't feel that they have anything to say, so they won't engage with feedback either.

Some ideas about employee engagement also point towards its fluctuating nature, noting that it isn't possible to be engaged all the time and that levels of engagement, motivation or job satisfaction may ebb and flow depending on a whole range of factors both inside and outside work. This means that if you ask people how they feel about their job, they might give different answers at different times.

It is also difficult to identify what 'good' engagement looks like, and the answer to this may be different for every organization. For example, an engaged lawyer in a particular firm might look different to an engaged nurse in a hospital. Another challenge is how we define 'good'. Some organizations might decide to put a certain percentage on engagement and use this as the definition of a good level, such as a high response to a question in a survey (which we discuss more later). There is no single way to identify if an organization has an engaged workforce, and no percentage that should be aimed for. Some people say that you know engagement when you see it – this might have some truth in it, but it would be difficult to turn that into an action plan!

Despite these challenges, listening to the employee voice, and trying to understand both how people feel about their work and how the employee experience can be improved, are all worthwhile goals. The challenges, however, should be noted and considered when analysing results and drafting action plans.

Measures

Questions that seek to measure engagement are often included in employee engagement surveys, which we will discuss more in the next section. In Chapter 1, we discussed the Utrecht definition of work engagement, which identifies engagement as being related to vigour, dedication and absorption. This research also identifies a set of questions and a scale that can provide employers with a formal measure of engagement. These include questions that employees can answer on a scale, such as:

• How energetic do employees feel at work?
• How proud do employees feel of their work?
• How inspired are employees by their job?

Other scales measure commitment, motivation or job satisfaction, many of which have been developed through academic research. Some scales seek to place a numerical measure on issues that might cause demotivation or disengagement, such as how stressed or burned-out people feel. Some specialist providers of employee engagement surveys may have developed their own methodologies for measuring engagement, or they may also use those developed by researchers.

There is no single 'best' way to measure or understand engagement, only the one that helps you to understand the information you are seeking. For example, if you want to measure stress, you will need a stress measurement tool. If you want to understand why people leave your organization, you will need to use exit interview data.

No single method of capturing feedback or understanding engagement can capture every aspect of what makes people happy, committed, satisfied or motivated. A formal measure can just be a starting point in understanding how people feel about their work and workplaces.

Challenges with obtaining feedback

Seeking to understand and measure how employees feel can be a very useful activity. But it can also be a challenging one. Below are a few of the challenges that organizations and HR professionals may experience.

PARTICIPATION BARRIERS

Not all employees will want to provide feedback about their experiences at work or how satisfied they are. This may stem from concerns about confidentiality or career impact. Some employees may not see the value of participating or be sceptical that it will result in meaningful change. Such scepticism often stems from a history of unaddressed feedback or a lack of visible action following previous surveys.

Lack of participation may also result from disengagement or practicalities such as lack of time or accessibility issues.

MANAGER BUY-IN

The success of an employee survey often depends on manager support, as they play a key role in promoting participation and passing on important messages about confidentiality. Managers who do not see the benefits of employee feedback may fail to encourage their teams to participate or even subtly undermine feedback mechanisms. Securing manager buy-in requires clear communication about how employee feedback may benefit them and their team members. Providing managers with training to interpret and act on survey results can also strengthen their commitment.

TIME AND RESOURCES

To measure and understand employee engagement at an in-depth level requires significant investment in time and potentially financial resources. HR professionals, leaders and managers will need to be involved at different stages. These might include deciding on and designing the approach to the feedback, analysing results and determining action plans and then implementing any agreed changes. This process can be resource-intensive, particularly for smaller organizations or those with limited budgets.

HONESTY BARRIERS
Employees may hesitate to provide honest feedback, especially feedback that is negative, due to concerns about anonymity and potential damage to themselves and their careers. This lack of honesty can undermine the reliability of data and prevent organizations from identifying genuine issues.

> **STOP AND THINK**
>
> Can you identify any potential barriers to gaining feedback from employees when seeking to measure engagement levels in your organization? Make a list of these barriers and how might they be overcome.

Employee surveys

> **Employee engagement survey:** A survey used by organizations to assess how employees feel about their work or their employer.

Organizations often undertake surveys to understand how employees feel about their jobs. These are typically called 'engagement' surveys, but some of them will go beyond just simply seeking to measure engagement and will look for broader feedback too.

Some organizations will undertake these surveys themselves; others will engage external survey providers to do it on their behalf. Surveys vary in terms of length, questions and whether they seek to determine an overall engagement 'measure' – often reflected as a percentage. Many will use quantitative questions, such as those that allow employees to rate how they feel about particular issues on a scale. Some will also use qualitative, open-ended questions that allow employees to provide more detailed feedback. An example of an open-ended survey question would be: 'What would you most like to change about our organization?'.

It is common to use the same questions regularly to identify trends, make comparisons with previous data and see if action plans are making a difference.

A well-designed survey can provide valuable insight into employee perceptions, risks and where improvements to the employee experience can be made.

EXERCISE

Does your organization currently undertake an engagement survey? If so, can you access the outcomes from previous surveys? If you can, familiarize yourself with the questions asked, and the key findings. Try to answer the following questions:

- What do your employees like about working for you?
- What would your employees like to change about working for you?

Survey design

HR professionals may contribute to survey design, communicating the survey and encouraging participation. There are several important considerations for employee engagement surveys:

- What does the organization need to know? What are the overall aims of the survey? For example, is it just to assess engagement, or do they want to welcome other feedback, suggestions or ideas for improvement? A survey should always have a goal.

- How can employees be encouraged to participate? Are there any barriers to participation that need to be addressed to maximize opportunities for completion? How can the survey be inclusive and accessible to everyone?
- How can employees be assured of anonymity and confidentiality so that they can provide feedback freely and honestly? This is key to receiving honest feedback.

When planning a survey, also think about how feedback will be acted upon and how the outcomes of the survey, and any resulting action plan, will be communicated to employees and managers.

A good employee engagement survey will also include some of the following:

- Demographic questions so that differences between employee groups can be identified and action plans can be tailored to meet specific employee needs.
- Categories for managerial and non-managerial employees, so that any differences between these two key groups can be identified.
- Some open-ended (or qualitative) questions to allow employees to provide feedback in their own words.

Well-designed surveys also ensure that:

- Questions are easy to understand, using plain language and simple vocabulary so that questions are accessible and not misunderstood.
- There aren't too many questions – there is no 'right' length, but if a survey is too long people might drop out; a good survey length is no more than around ten minutes.
- Any rating scales that are used are simply explained. For example, if you are asking employees to rate how they feel

using a scale of 1–5, make it clear whether 5 is the highest or lowest score.

Engagement surveys are often undertaken online, although it is important to consider if different options are needed to capture all employees. This is especially important if you have a workforce that does not typically work at a desk, for example, those that incorporate remote, field or shift workers. Consider whether you need alternative methods like paper surveys or mobile-friendly platforms.

Encouraging participation

As we discussed in the previous section, a range of factors may influence employee participation in feedback, including taking part in employee engagement surveys. There are also particular challenges with participation in surveys. Not everyone will complete them, and those who do complete them may not be honest about how they feel about their work or their employer. They can also only provide a snapshot of the organization at a given moment. Each employee who completes it does so based on their feelings at that time, and these feelings may change and evolve. Despite these challenges, surveys can still be an important tool for organizations and HR professionals, so they are worth pursuing. Identifying these potential problems and having a plan to address them can help to ensure that the maximum benefit is derived from a survey exercise.

To overcome any practical barriers to taking part, participation should be made as easy and convenient as possible, such as offering different options or formats, or scheduling time during work hours to take part. Ensure that you take the following steps:

- Raise awareness – ensure that all employees are aware of the survey, why it is being done and what participation involves. Communication should be regular, use a variety of different methods and include any hard-to-reach employee groups.

- Share benefits – employees may be more likely to participate if they can see what is in it for them. Benefits could include long-term improvements or addressing problems or concerns that are highlighted.
- Emphasize confidentiality – employees should be given assurances about confidentiality and anonymity in any surveys. If necessary, include a statement about how this is achieved, including any protocols that an external provider is using.
- Demonstrate past actions – show previous surveys that have led to change, improvements or addressed past problems. This will help employees to recognize that the time they put into the survey can have a direct benefit.

Some organizations also incentivize taking part, such as donating to charity if a threshold is met or contributing in some way to a cause important to employees or the organization itself. For example, one organization planted a tree for every completed survey via a carbon offsetting programme.

Using employee engagement data to drive change

Employee engagement data, whether from a survey or other method of employee voice, should provide the organization, and its HR professionals, with valuable data that can drive action and change. The process begins with analysing the data.

Analysing data

There are many ways to analyse employee survey data:

- Qualitative data, such as information from focus groups or open-ended questions, can be read and organized into key themes. Software packages exist that can help with this, and there are lots of simple ways to present this data, such as word clouds highlighting word frequency.

- Quantitative data can be analysed using statistical methods to identify trends, correlations and areas of concern. This typically involves calculating metrics such as averages and percentages that provide a snapshot of employee sentiment. Advanced techniques like regression analysis or factor analysis can also be applied to provide a more in-depth picture. Visualizations such as bar graphs, pie charts and heatmaps are commonly used to communicate findings.

If you use an external partner to undertake a survey for you, they will typically do much of the initial analysis. If you are analysing the data, here are a few things to look out for:

- If you have undertaken a previous survey, how do scores compare with previous years – what has gone up overall and what has gone down?
- Are there any departments or areas of the organization where scores are very different, either to each other or to overall scores? Can you identify any reason for this?
- Are there specific survey questions that consistently receive low scores, indicating areas that need targeted attention or improvement?
- Do any demographic groups show significant variations in their answers, which should be further investigated? These could suggest equality or inclusion issues.

TIP

If your organization currently undertakes an employee engagement survey, look at the questions it asks. Are they qualitative or quantitative? Do employees get the opportunity to provide any open-ended feedback on the things that matter to them? Open questions allow employees to say what matters to them at work in their own words and can provide useful insight for HR professionals.

Sharing feedback with employees

Survey feedback should always be shared with employees. A good approach is to communicate organization-wide feedback and key findings with everyone. There are lots of ways to do this, from creating infographics, leader briefings or even blogs, vlogs or podcasts.

Once decided, it is also a good idea to share the main focus areas based on the feedback. This could be the top three to five priority areas.

Leaders and managers can then be provided with data for their specific areas of responsibility, allowing for a cascade of more detailed and relevant information. Training managers to understand and use survey data effectively can also amplify the benefits of engagement initiatives, ensuring that the results lead to actionable insights rather than just a collection of statistics. They can then be encouraged to share the results with their own teams and facilitate discussions about improvement and change.

Acting on feedback

It is important to act upon feedback, whatever approach you have taken to gather it. One common method for updating employees is 'you said, we did'. This simple framework links employer actions to employee feedback, stating what has been done or what is planned. There may be times that feedback cannot be acted upon, perhaps because it is not appropriate or because there are resource constraints. It's a good idea to let people know if there is feedback that you cannot action, and why.

Being transparent about feedback and sharing action plans can help to build a culture of trust across the organization. It can also help to ensure that employees feel that contributing feedback is a worthwhile exercise, as the organization is listening and willing to act.

> **TIP**
>
> Sometimes, feedback might need further investigation, or a problem will be raised that does not have a clear solution. See this as an opportunity to create employee involvement and more scope for employee voice. Consider running focus groups or interviews to take a deep dive into the issue and crowdsource ideas for change.

Action planning for change

Once employee engagement survey results are analysed, organizations should create actionable plans to address the feedback received. This is likely to include addressing any problems or issues highlighted, but can also include how to further improve areas identified as strong. Here are a few things to think about:

- Based on the feedback received, what are the priority areas? Where can you gain the maximum benefit from your time and resources? It is never possible to tackle everything that is raised in feedback, and nor should you necessarily try to do so. Be guided by key themes, but also by where you will gain the most impact.
- Can you engage employees in the action-planning process? This will help to further support employee voice, provide a way to 'test' ideas with the people potentially most affected by them, and foster a sense of ownership.
- Make sure any goals or objectives set are SMART – specific, measurable, achievable, relevant and time-bound. Every action should have a deadline and key measures of success.
- Establish mechanisms for checking on progress, adjusting plans where needed and helping to maintain momentum. Having someone with overall responsibility for the plan and each of its elements will help to support accountability.

There may need to be an organization-wide action plan, and then plans that sit at a local or departmental level. When feedback is shared and cascaded effectively, this will help to ensure local planning and action take place. There should always be a way that local action plans feed back to leaders or owners, to ensure that action is sustained and aligned to broader organizational initiatives.

HR professionals can support this entire process in several ways. They can facilitate the creation of the action plan, taking ownership of elements that might sit within their areas of responsibility, such as the employment lifecycle (discussed in Chapter 7). They can work with managers to help them analyse their local data, develop department or team action plans and provide advice on focus areas and opportunities for change. Remember – HR is a department in its own right, so may also need a local action plan that relates to their own teams, as well as supporting and facilitating wider engagement efforts. HR professionals are also employees and have their own employee experience.

CHAPTER SUMMARY

- Listening to employee perspectives can lead to improvements in the organization that leaders might not think of themselves. It helps people to feel listened to and valued, making them more engaged and less likely to quit.

- Organizations can gather feedback through mechanisms such as employee surveys, focus groups, pulse surveys, engaging with trade unions and analysing social media data.

- It can be challenging to measure engagement – not every employee will want to participate in providing feedback.

- Employee surveys are a common method of understanding employee attitudes and feelings about their work and organization. If well-designed, implemented and utilized, they can be an effective tool for change.

- Employers must act upon information received from employees; through sharing information they can ensure transparency and build trust, while creating a culture conducive to sharing and feedback.
- HR professionals can support the processes of understanding and measuring engagement, taking both a practical role in organizing or administering feedback mechanisms, and helping with analysing data, communication and action planning for improvement.

REVIEW QUESTIONS

1 Identify some of the signs that an employee might be disengaged at work.

2 Make a list of different ways that an organization can seek to understand or measure employee engagement.

3 Name at least one challenge that HR may have to overcome when undertaking an employee engagement survey.

Further reading

CIPD report (2021) Employee engagement – definitions, measures and outcomes, www.cipd.org/globalassets/media/knowledge/knowledge-hub/evidence-reviews/employee-engagement-discussion-report_tcm18-89598.pdf (archived at https://perma.cc/7FM8-S5YE)

Endnote

1 www.mckinsey.com/capabilities/people-and-organizational-performance/our-insights/how-to-identify-employee-disengagement (archived at https://perma.cc/FW6H-8Q28)

CHAPTER FOUR

Increasing engagement

Introduction

We have identified why employee engagement matters to organizations, what drives and enables employee engagement, and how we can understand how people think and feel about their work through a range of different employee voice methods.

Many organizations and managers are understandably interested in increasing employee engagement to maximize its business benefits. In this chapter, we discuss how organizations can do this, from practical quick wins to longer-term strategies around issues such as organizational culture. We also explore what might get in the way when seeking to improve employee engagement, such as practical barriers to engagement during difficult times.

> **LEARNING OBJECTIVES**
>
> By the end of this chapter, you will be able to:
>
> - Explain different approaches to improving employee engagement.
> - Identify quick-win, practical and cost-effective activities to boost engagement.

- Put strategies in place to support the cultural change necessary to increase engagement.
- Recognize barriers to increasing engagement.
- Explain some key HR activities that can increase engagement.

Increasing engagement

Although, as we saw in Chapter 1, it can be difficult to define exactly what we mean by employee engagement, and it can be difficult to precisely measure it, many people would agree that aiming to increase it can have positive outcomes for employees and organizations.

Improving people's working experience is undoubtedly a good thing for them as individuals and for their organizations. There is increasing interest (including from governments and campaigning organizations) in the idea of 'good work'. Although this can mean different things to different people, it typically refers to issues such as strong employment protections, job security, fair wages and income security, working conditions, inclusion and opportunity. Good work benefits employees and organizations, as well as society as a whole and the economy. There is considerable cross-over between what amounts to good work and the factors that can drive individual employee engagement.

To increase engagement in an organization, employers can broadly take two different approaches – when combined these will form the best platform for change. We consider both of these approaches in this chapter:

1 Focus on what we already know drives and supports engagement, using some of the research discussed previously in this book. This evidence base can help us to determine where to spend time and resources and understand the potential

benefits. Suggestions and recommendations for using this existing evidence base follow later in this chapter.

2 Following the guidance and recommendations in Chapter 3, organizations can use the specific feedback provided by their employees through employee voice mechanisms, which are often more focused on the organization's unique culture. These feelings, perceptions and ideas can provide valuable, context-specific insight that can be leveraged for change.

Whichever approach is taken (and combining the two is likely to provide the best results), increasing engagement generally requires a long-term strategy – although there are beneficial quick actions you can take, too.

Many of the factors that influence engagement are interconnected. Any strategy for increasing engagement will need to recognize this; focusing on one aspect of engagement might be useful and result in positive outcomes, but to truly leverage engagement, organizations and their HR teams will need to address multiple elements and drivers.

Quick wins for employee engagement

Engagement is something that builds over time and is an accumulation of many experiences over the employment lifecycle. It is made up of lots of different interactions and is influenced by different factors. Quick fixes will not necessarily shift overall sentiment significantly overnight. However, there are quick wins and short-term actions that can help to support employee engagement building over time and will help to improve the employee experience. Quick wins should be introduced with caution. For example, timing is important. Employees may take a cynical view if you introduce activities just before your annual engagement survey. Following are some examples of quick wins that support employee engagement:

- Introduce organizational-specific methods for recognizing achievement, good performance and employee effort.
- Celebrate employee milestones. This can mean work anniversaries but may also include acknowledging and celebrating employees' birthdays, major life events or their achievements outside of work.
- Conduct stay interviews. Ask employees what keeps them motivated, what they enjoy about their role, and what improvements they'd like. This helps HR address issues before they lead to disengagement.
- Host social activities. Not everyone will want to participate, but many people value the relationships that they have with colleagues. Activities can be simple and inexpensive, such as providing an occasional lunch or coffee morning. Such activities provide opportunities to connect and build relationships, which are good for engagement. We delve into this point in a little more depth later in the chapter.
- Share regular updates from leaders. Have leaders share short, regular updates on the organization's performance, successes and challenges. Transparent communication makes employees feel included and valued. Give people the opportunity to ask questions in informal sessions too, if possible.
- Provide good tea, coffee and lots of fresh water. Meeting people's basic needs is relatively inexpensive but can make the working day more pleasant.
- Consider the physical work environment. Where people work matters, and paying attention to the work environment sends a clear signal about the extent to which they are valued. Not all changes to the physical work environment need to be expensive – think about comfort, light and creating relaxing places to meet others.
- Long service awards. Recognizing service allows organizations to acknowledge contributions that employees have made over time and can help to build loyalty.

- Introduce career development conversations. Employees are motivated by opportunities to learn and develop. Providing opportunities for career discussion and development planning helps engage employees, as it helps them to see their future with the organization and increases their sense of belonging.
- Provide a mechanism for employees to make suggestions for improvement. This contributes to the idea of employee voice. Employees will often have a range of ideas about how the organization can work more effectively but may need to be expressly encouraged to voice them. When employees contribute in this way, it supports engagement and may lead to good organizational outcomes.

Creating the right culture

Organizational culture is another term used in HR and management that can be defined and interpreted differently. It's commonly described as 'how things are done around here'. While this is a relatively simple definition, it encompasses many things – how people behave, the norms, beliefs and values of the organization, the stories people tell about it, and generally how it feels to work there. There are visible elements of culture, too, such as the physical working environment or how people dress at work.

All organizations have a unique culture, which is typically influenced by people, leaders, industry, history, values and external forces. Culture develops over time, and it can be passively allowed to do so, or organizations (and HR professionals) can take a more proactive, strategic approach to it.

If we want high levels of employee engagement, we need to create an organizational culture capable of delivering it. Although engagement and culture are different things, they are interlinked in many ways. For example, it will be difficult to have a great working culture and employee engagement if people are treated or managed poorly, if there are high levels of stress or unpleasant working environments, or where bullying or blame is part of the everyday experience. Engaged employees form an important part of creating a great culture; people who are (depending on your preferred definition of engagement) vigorous, enthusiastic, committed and motivated will often bring that into their behaviours and relationships at work – positively influencing culture as individuals.

There is a cross-over between the steps that support culture, the elements that drive employee experience (discussed in Chapter 1) and employee engagement. How people are treated through the employment lifecycle, discussed later in this chapter, is connected to culture, as these are key stages for many people in their working lives with an employer.

Building a culture of engagement is a long-term strategy; culture can rarely be changed quickly. Creating culture demands two things:

1 An understanding of where you are now (which can be achieved through the activities discussed in Chapter 3). This is broader than how engaged someone is at work and incorporates what people believe and say about their organization. It relates to understanding all the ways that things are done within the organization.

2 A clear vision of where you want to be in the future: what does 'good' mean to you in your context? What would an engaged culture look like? What would be different from today? Having a 'why' provides focus and direction.

Without the latter element, it is impossible to know whether you have been successful or not, and engagement activities may end up unfocused or disjointed.

> **STOP AND THINK**
>
> Organizational culture is often described as 'the way we do things around here'. How would you describe the culture of your organization? Is the culture conducive to high employee engagement?

We can build a culture of engagement through some of the engagement drivers we identified in Chapter 2. While each strategy for increasing engagement is unique and should always be tailored to the organization's own context and goals, some of the drivers for increasing engagement should be considered for inclusion in any plan.

To help you think about your organization, we will now briefly return to some of those drivers and consider options for improvement. For each one, consider what steps your organization could take to improve the current processes and ways of working. What initiatives or activities might increase employee engagement and improve culture? Use the reflection questions to help you; where you find it difficult to answer the question or answer it in the negative, these may be areas that you would want to include in a future employee engagement strategy.

Work-life balance

> **Work-life balance:** An employee's personal, optimal balance between their work and the non-work elements of their lives.

Work-life balance increasingly matters to employees – sometimes more than salary or financial rewards. One 2024 survey, carried out by the global talent company Ransdstad, found that 83 per cent of employees felt work-life balance was their key motivator.[1] What matters to employees will show up in the decisions they make about where they work and how satisfied they are. Expectations about work-life balance, especially any that arise during the recruitment process, will form part of the psychological contract. Work-life balance is influenced by the broader culture of the organization. If employees believe that work-life balance is valued and recognized as important, and if the ways of working within the organization itself support work-life balance, this will contribute to both positive culture and employee engagement. When people can work in a way that works for them as individuals, balancing their style and preference with other responsibilities, this will also support their health, motivation, productivity and retention.

Work-life balance can be influenced positively through formal HR policies, especially those relating to time off, family leave and flexible work arrangements – all of which are discussed later in this chapter. It can also be improved through wellbeing programmes, our other key topic in this book, and the messages that the organization and its managers send. This might mean express messaging, such as encouragement to take breaks or more implicit messaging, such as what or who gets rewarded and why.

STOP AND THINK

- What do people believe about work-life balance in your organization?

- Do your current HR policies and processes support work-life balance? How do your policies benchmark against those of other organizations?

- Does any element of your culture reward long working hours or presenteeism?

- Can your employees effectively switch off from work – and work technology?

Colleague relationships

Many people value the connections they have with people at work, building meaningful relationships with colleagues. Liking the people you work with can be a powerful driver of engagement and the day-to-day experience of work. For some, affiliation is a powerful motivator. Strong colleague relationships contribute to a sense of belonging and facilitate collaboration and teamwork; they can also act as a buffer against stress or work demands. It is therefore in organizations' interests to support and facilitate good working relationships, deliberately connecting people across teams and functions, removing silos and simply providing space for people to get to know each other. Good relationships are also defined by addressing issues fairly and promptly, such as conflict within teams.

Organizations can take steps to develop strong working relationships between colleagues, and many of them are relatively inexpensive. Simple (voluntary) social activities like coffee mornings, hobby groups or lunch clubs can all help to connect people who might not otherwise get to know one another. Teams can incorporate team building or networking elements into meetings or events. There are also opportunities within the physical working environment to facilitate connection, such as creating comfortable common areas or break rooms where people can relax and chat. Internal networking groups can also connect people and provide valuable support, especially for those experiencing similar challenges or life or career stages. Examples could be a working parents' group, a disabled staff group, a carers' group, or a network for interns and recent graduates.

STOP AND THINK

- Does your organization offer sufficient opportunities for employees to interact and build relationships, such as team-building activities, social events or networking?

- Do leaders and managers encourage meaningful connections within their teams – and beyond?
- Would employees think that it was acceptable for them to take time to focus on building working relationships?

Vision and values

Vision: A statement that clearly sets out the future goals of the organization.

Values: The stated core beliefs or principles held by an organization, intended to guide action and provide purpose and direction.

An organization's vision or values can be a powerful way to direct organizational culture and activity. The vision should indicate a direction of travel for employees and provide insight into where they fit in and how they can contribute. Values are more about the 'how'. They describe what an organization stands for and its beliefs. Values should set the culture by providing principles to follow. Unfortunately, values often fall short of this lofty goal. Instead, they are designed but then somewhat forgotten, and they do not get sufficiently talked about or embedded into day-to-day working life. Values can be undermined if there are no consequences for not adhering to them. When values are embedded into practice and 'lived' by managers and employees, they can support both culture and engagement. Values are linked to purpose, another driver of engagement, helping to make work meaningful. Organizational values are a particularly powerful force for engagement when they align with an employee's own values.

How values are communicated is important. They should be prominent and reinforced often. This is about more than putting them on the wall and website; it is about discussing and aligning with the employment lifecycle. For example, values should be discussed in interviews and performance reviews. Managers should be encouraged to incorporate conversations about values into their day-to-day practice and meetings with their team. Reward and recognition can be aligned to demonstrated values, and behaviour that is misaligned with organizational values should be quickly addressed.

STOP AND THINK

- How effectively does your organization communicate its values to employees? Would most employees be able to name them?

- Do your employees see leaders 'living' your values, or are there gaps between stated values and what happens in practice?

- Are your values aligned with your HR practices?

- What could be done to help employees better understand how their work contributes to the broader organizational vision and mission?

Voice

As we have already seen, employee voice plays an important role in engagement and culture and it is one of the primary drivers of engagement, according to Engage for Success (discussed in Chapter 2). Employees will only speak up if it is safe to do so within the organization's culture. Effective voice mechanisms will not only surface potential problems, but give scope for employees to make suggestions and contribute to the organization's success. We discussed the different ways to do this in

Chapter 3, as well as how to act upon the feedback that is received. Ideally, organizations will have a structured approach to listening to employee voice, whatever their size and resources.

STOP AND THINK

- Do you think that your employees feel comfortable sharing their ideas, concerns and feedback openly?

- Do you have formal mechanisms (such as those discussed in Chapter 3) for your employees to provide input and feedback? How do you know if they are working?

- Do you have a formal listening strategy that ensures the employee voice is heard and acted upon? What do you do with the information that employees provide to you?

WHAT WOULD YOU DO?
Number 3

Imagine a manager tells you they think engagement is generally low within their whole team. They don't have any specific evidence, but they sense people feel unhappy and demotivated. They want to take action to boost engagement and motivation, and ask you for some suggestions.

- What questions would you ask of this manager so you can understand the issue fully?

- What advice would you give them, and what recommendations would you make?

- How would your advice differ from addressing a single disengaged employee in Chapter 3?

Consider both the quick wins and longer-term strategies when formulating your answer.

Barriers to increasing engagement

A range of barriers can get in the way of increasing employee engagement, including:

• resource or budget constraints
• a lack of appetite to make the necessary changes
• a lack of leadership buy-in

Some of the factors that decrease engagement might be quite difficult to influence as they are not within the control of the organization. There can also be cultural factors at play or competing organizational priorities. Increasing employee engagement is rarely something that can be achieved overnight. Quick wins can make a difference in employee sentiment, but many of the changes that influence engagement positively may take a long time to result in tangible benefits.

> **STOP AND THINK**
>
> What barriers to engagement can you identify that are specific to your organization, culture and the work that people do? Can you suggest any ways that these barriers can be overcome?

Building engagement through HR activities

As well as the quick wins and the longer-term strategies we have discussed in this chapter so far, there are other practical and everyday ways that HR professionals can support employee engagement. Based on what we know can drive both engagement and employee experience, we will now discuss some activities and programmes specific to the work of HR that can build it, as well as support some of the broader strategic areas set out above.

STOP AND THINK

Reflect on the activities and programmes discussed in this section. Which of these does your organization already do? If you don't currently do them, could they help you to improve your employee engagement?

Recognition schemes

Recognition schemes can play an important role in acknowledging and rewarding employees' hard work and achievements. These programs can range from formal awards ceremonies to more informal gestures like small thank-you gifts or shout-outs in meetings. A common recognition scheme is 'employee of the month'. Ideally, these schemes should be tailored to align with company values or organizational objectives and goals.

Employee volunteering

Volunteering programmes can bring several benefits to organizations and employees. Programmes can align with organizational goals around sustainability or social responsibility. They can be good for the organization's brand, but they can also support employees to develop new skills. Volunteering can take many forms. Some organizations allow employees an amount of time that they can use for volunteering of their choosing. Others support a particular charity and organize specific events or activities for them. From an engagement perspective, volunteering can help employees find purpose and meaning in their work. It can help to retain employees for whom volunteering is important.

Flexible benefits

Flexible benefits programmes typically offer employees the freedom to tailor their benefits packages to meet their individual needs or life stage. Schemes work in different ways, but typically they provide employees with a benefits amount that they can 'spend' on different benefits from childcare to a savings account. Flexible benefits recognize that different employees have different priorities and motivators, so allowing them to choose the benefits that matter to them can help to support engagement and broader talent management goals (attracting and retaining employees).

Mentoring programmes

Mentoring typically refers to a one-to-one relationship between employees and more experienced individuals. The mentor can act as a guide, either from a general career perspective or with a focus on a development area or goal. Mentoring is a form of development – a key motivator and contributor to employee engagement.

Flexible working

The opportunity to work flexibly can be highly valued by employees – sometimes more than monetary rewards. Work can be flexible in time or place and can take forms such as remote or hybrid work, part-time working, job shares or a four-day week. Offering whatever flexible forms of work suit your organization can be a valuable driver for employee engagement, including attraction and retention of talent. Flexible working can often be provided at no or low cost to organizations.

Support at key life stages

Throughout their lives, and therefore their employment, employees naturally have major life events from having children to menopause to retirement. These life stages will affect employees in different ways, and organizations can reflect this through policies and support. For example, comprehensive family policies, adjustments for employees experiencing menopause or help with retirement planning all help to create a positive work environment where employees feel supported, thereby improving their psychological state.

Diversity and inclusion initiatives

There are strong moral and legal arguments for organizations to focus on diversity, equality and inclusion. There are engagement impacts, too. Inclusion can help people to feel like they belong and that they can be themselves. Environments that lack diversity, or where there are issues like discrimination or harassment, are not conducive to situations in which employees can be happy and give their best to their work. Diversity initiatives vary significantly but can include targeted for underrepresented groups, inclusion training for managers, employment policies that promote inclusion, networking groups or pay and equality audits. Many of these activities would fall under the remit of HR departments, sometimes working with people managers.

Learning and development

Opportunities to develop are key to engagement and motivation. They also contribute to the creation of a skilled and effective workforce and, therefore, have multiple benefits to organizations. Employees want to be able to grow and learn – and as we shall see later, the ability to learn also supports employee wellbeing. Learning and development can take many forms, from formal training to some of the elements discussed previously, such as mentoring or career conversations. Learning provision will depend on job needs and the organization's resources, but its contribution to employee engagement should not be overlooked.

Leadership training and development

Managers have a significant impact on employee engagement through how they manage employees day-to-day. There are many reasons to develop people managers, but ensuring that this group of employees understands their role in engagement and the employee experience (as well as wellbeing!) is an important one. Providing managers with skills and understanding about how they can influence engagement, both positively and negatively, can help to ensure that engagement is treated seriously and embedded into the organization, going beyond HR initiatives and activities.

STOP AND THINK

Which of the HR activities listed here are undertaken or offered by your organization?

Identify any gaps or areas where these policies or practices could be improved to help support employee engagement and employee experience.

Engagement during difficult times

From time to time, organizations may need to make difficult decisions concerning their workforce. These might include a need for redundancies, downsizing or change programmes that will not be welcomed by employees. Such programmes are often managed by HR professionals, which can conflict with their responsibilities towards employee engagement. In difficult times, employees may feel demotivated, unhappy or unable to give their best. Job insecurity or fear of forthcoming change are not ingredients for an engaged workforce.

However, it is still important to think about employee engagement even when times are hard. How such situations are handled can have a long-term effect on engagement levels but will be less damaging to long-term employee sentiment and engagement if they are well-managed and seen to be fair and transparent. Keep in mind some of the following if you are involved in difficult HR programmes of work:

- Provide employees with timely, honest and clear information about what is going on and the reasons behind the decisions that have been taken. Messages should be delivered by senior leaders wherever possible. Transparency builds trust, even in difficult times.
- Offer practical and emotional support to affected employees. This could include mental health support or (in the case of redundancies) career transition or job-seeking support. Remember that it is not just employees who are directly affected by redundancy or downsizing and who might need support, but also their colleagues.
- Equip managers to communicate effectively, answer questions and provide reassurance to their teams, providing them with the necessary training or guidance. Managers are often the first point of contact for questions so should be supported accordingly. Providing timely answers to employee concerns and questions will also help to manage emotions and indicate transparency.
- When the work is at an end, communicate this. For example, in the event of restructuring, confirm that there are no further actions to be taken.

After the programme or activity has formally concluded, emotions can take time to settle and fears can remain. Continue to provide support as necessary.

WHAT WOULD YOU DO?
Number 4

Your organization is having to make redundancies in one area of the business where there is a downturn in work. However, in another area, where business is going well, you must ensure employees are motivated and engaged to hit targets.

- How can you sensitively recognize or reward the efforts of employees in the thriving area to keep their motivation high?

- What advice would you give to the manager of the group that needs to be engaged and motivated?

- Name three simple steps the company could take to support engagement during this time.

Use the content in this chapter to help you with your response.

Engagement with hybrid and remote teams

From time to time, external or internal factors will affect the workplace and necessitate change. Technological change, economic change, societal change or political change – all of these can have an impact on individual organizations and, more generally, on work and how it is done.

Hybrid work: A work pattern that involves working some time remotely (usually from home) and some time from a workplace (typically an office).

The Covid-19 pandemic is an example of this. During the pandemic, many thousands of employees globally were required to work from home. As a result, flexible work became more common. Some form of hybrid work is now undertaken by around a quarter of workers around the world. Changes of this kind require HR professionals to adapt; when they do so, they can add value and impact. They can be proactive, seizing new opportunities that will help organizations reach their goals through their people. They may also need to adapt policies and processes, support people managers with these changes, and learn new forms of good practice. The shift to hybrid work is an example of why HR professionals always need to keep learning, adapting and looking toward the future. We will return more to this idea in the book's Conclusion.

Hybrid and remote work present new challenges for engaging employees, as some of the key activities that form part of employee engagement may need to be adapted for this different way of working. Hybrid and remote workers naturally spend less time working in a physical workplace together, so their experience of work and the workplace is different. This does not necessarily mean, as some people fear, that they will be less engaged or productive, but it does mean that the organization needs to adapt its approach.

HR professionals and people managers must consider some of the following concerning employee engagement and flexible workers:

- How to ensure that key elements of the employee lifecycle, such as induction, can be adapted to ensure that they are effective in a hybrid or remote environment.
- How to keep employees connected to their colleagues, maximizing the importance of social connection for engagement and wellbeing.
- How to implement regular and meaningful communication practices that prevent remote workers from feeling isolated or disconnected. This may include the use of relevant workplace technologies.
- How to ensure equal access to development opportunities and career progression for remote and hybrid workers.
- How to foster a sense of belonging and inclusion among hybrid and remote workers, ensuring that, regardless of location, all employees feel connected to the organizational culture and its values.
- How to support employee well-being and mental health in environments where physical cues of stress or burnout may be less visible.

To support engagement in hybrid and remote teams, HR professionals should review each of these areas and assess the extent to which current ways of working fit hybrid, remote and flexible workers. In addition, they can:

- seek out opportunities to increase connection with culture and colleagues
- look for new ways to communicate
- help employees get the learning and development they need

Consider whether it would be useful to talk directly to these employees to gain insights from them, as well as ideas for improvement. Critically, plans should include supporting managers to adapt their management style to these changes.

STOP AND THINK

Think about what you have learned about employee engagement so far.

- Has your understanding of employee engagement changed? If so, how?
- Were you surprised by any criticisms of employee engagement? Why, or why not?

CHAPTER SUMMARY

- Organizations can take two different approaches to increasing engagement. They can use the existing evidence base and/or their own data gathered from surveys and other sources of feedback provided through employee voice mechanisms. Combining these approaches will result in the most positive change.

- Some quick wins that are part of the employment lifecycle can help support broader and more strategic engagement interventions.

- Engagement is influenced by organizational culture, especially factors such as work-life balance and healthy colleague relationships.
- Numerous barriers can get in the way of increasing engagement. It's a good idea to familiarize yourself with any that exist in your organization.
- Employee engagement can be supported through HR activities, policies and initiatives.

REVIEW QUESTIONS

1 Define organizational culture. What does it include?

2 Explain why an organization may want to increase employee engagement.

3 Identify a quick win for increasing employee engagement that you could recommend introducing to your manager.

4 Name two barriers that an organization may face when trying to improve employee engagement.

Further reading

Mitchel, D (2017) *50 Top Tools for Employee Engagement: A complete toolkit for improving motivation and productivity*, Kogan Page

Endnote

1   https://www.randstad.com/workmonitor/#:~:text=explore%20the%20 themes%20for%202025.&text=And%20for%20the%20first%20 time,other%20ways%20to%20feel%20fulfillment (archived at https://perma.cc/5M2E-8CCF)

CHAPTER FIVE

Introducing wellbeing

Introduction

Just like employee engagement, employee health and wellbeing are of great interest and importance to employers. This chapter begins by considering just what we mean when we talk about employee wellbeing, as well as other related concepts, including mental health, stress and burnout. A handy wellbeing terminology guide is included.

We also explore the organizational benefits of employee wellbeing and the business case for investing in it, as well as what can drive wellbeing at work and detract from it.

Although most people agree that organizations should take employee health and wellbeing seriously, there can be barriers that get in the way, and it can be difficult to identify what works in practice. We will briefly explore these before a more detailed review in Chapter 6.

Following on from discussions in Chapter 3 about measuring engagement, we also consider how organizations can seek to measure and understand the health and wellness of their employees.

LEARNING OBJECTIVES

By the end of this chapter, you will be able to:

- Define wellbeing and related terms including mental health and burnout.

- Explain why employee wellbeing is important for organizations and the rationale for investing in wellbeing.

- Articulate the main drivers and detractors of employee wellbeing.

- Describe the link between stress and mental health at work.

- Articulate some of the ways to measure wellbeing at work.

- Explain how HR professionals can influence culture so that it supports wellbeing.

- Articulate some criticisms of wellbeing programmes at work.

What is wellbeing?

Wellbeing: a holistic state of physical, mental and emotional health and overall life satisfaction, subjectively defined by the individual.

As with employee engagement, wellbeing is a term with many different definitions. It is in everyday use and is also used by academics undertaking research into health. It includes physical and mental health, but also other related ideas like work-life balance, burnout and resilience. Some definitions incorporate wider ideas of wellbeing, including financial and social health. Wellbeing is also linked to topics discussed in the first part of this book, including motivation, engagement and job satisfaction. For this reason, wellbeing is sometimes referred to as an umbrella term for a range of concepts.

Traditionally, it is thought that there are two different types of individual wellbeing: eudemonic and hedonic.

Eudemonic wellbeing: A definition of wellbeing that focuses on people's purpose, positive emotion and self-awareness.

Hedonic wellbeing: A definition of wellbeing that focuses on pleasure and happiness. It is sometimes also called subjective wellbeing.

The World Health Organization defines wellbeing as a positive state that encompasses quality of life, thriving and a sense of meaning and purpose.[1] Another helpful definition from the New Economics Foundation, a British think tank, describes wellbeing as 'feeling good and functioning well'.[2]

Workplace wellbeing can influence a range of organizational outcomes, some of which are particularly relevant to HR professionals, including absence, turnover, costs and productivity. It is also linked to our first subject in this book – employee engagement.

Work can have positive and negative influences on individual wellbeing. It can contribute to health through fulfilling people's social or esteem needs, or it can be a cause of stress. Despite this, not all organizations take a strategic or planned approach to wellbeing, and some only provide reactive support if someone is unwell.

Wellbeing terminology

Let's consider some key terms that are often used within the broader idea of wellbeing at work.

WORK-LIFE BALANCE

Work-life balance refers to the different aspects of people's lives, work and non-work, and the extent to which someone has found the balance that works for them. Just like with wellbeing, it is a term that means different things to different people – and ideas about what 'good' balance looks like can often vary over people's lives as their circumstances change. As we discussed in Chapter 3, work-life balance relates to employee engagement as well as overall wellbeing.

WORK-RELATED STRESS

Stress is generally considered to be a feeling of pressure and strain – especially when pressure is sustained for some time. It is a reaction – a bodily response to that feeling of pressure or threat. Everyone experiences some sort of stress at some point in their lives, and it is not necessarily always a problem. A small amount of stress can be helpful in some circumstances. Work-related stress is when this feeling of pressure relates to the pressures of work.

MENTAL HEALTH

The World Health Organization defines mental health as 'a state of wellbeing in which every individual realizes his or her own potential, can cope with the normal stresses of life, can work productively and fruitfully, and is able to make a contribution to her or his community'.[3] Everyone has mental health, and it can fluctuate on a spectrum from very good to very poor. Some people use the terms 'mental health problems' or 'mental illness'. These are umbrella terms that can be used to refer to common mental health conditions such as anxiety, depression or stress, or other rarer conditions such as bipolar disorder or eating disorders. Mental health disorders vary significantly in terms of symptoms and outcomes. Mental health problems affect around one in four people in any given year.

BURNOUT

Burnout is another term that is often used in everyday use – sometimes, people use it to mean that they are exhausted or overwhelmed. In a work context, it has a specific meaning. Burnout occurs when an individual has been suffering from long-term stress at work that has not been resolved. This can lead to symptoms including exhaustion, but also reduced feelings of personal efficacy, a loss of connection from work and feelings of negativity.

RESILIENCE

Resilience is often referred to as how people 'bounce back' after challenges or difficulties. In a workplace context, this could be how people respond to challenging or stressful work situations. Resilient employees are said to be able to cope with and adapt to workplace change and respond positively to high-pressure situations. Organizations are often interested in how to help employees become more resilient.

PRESENTEEISM

This term can refer to situations where employees work when perhaps they shouldn't, as they are concerned about how it will look if they take time off. An example might be someone who works when they are unwell. It might also refer to cultural pressure to 'be present' and visible in the workplace. Another related form is 'leavism' – working when on a form of leave. Presenteeism is often driven by organizational culture; it may also be perpetuated by people managers.

DIGITAL WELLBEING

This refers to the impact of technology on our overall health and wellbeing. It includes the potential for technology to support our health, but also its potential downsides. In a workplace context, it includes issues such as switching off from digital devices, the impact of prolonged screen use and what is sometimes known as 'technostress' – overload from using multiple digital technologies.

PSYCHOLOGICAL SAFETY

An organization or culture is said to be psychologically safe if people feel that it is okay to be themselves and to speak up – especially in the context of disagreeing – and to take risks. This is a narrower concept than wellbeing, but if employees have a good sense of safety, this is likely to also contribute to wellbeing in the workplace.

The business case for wellbeing

In the UK, the Department for Work and Pensions estimates that the total annual economic cost of ill-health is over £100bn. Every year, 131 million working days are lost due to employee sickness absence.

The UK CIPD has found that good employee wellbeing is associated with increased employee motivation and morale, as well as positive and inclusive organizational cultures and better work-life balance. These aren't the only benefits. Organizations that support the health and wellbeing of their employees will also typically see fewer accidents and sickness absences, as well as higher productivity. It is also good for reputation and employer brand, helping to attract and retain employees. These can all lead to positive financial outcomes for the organization.

In 2008, management consultancy Price Waterhouse Cooper identified that for every £1 an organization spends on workplace wellbeing, they saw a return of £4.17 in benefits.[4] Later research by Deloitte in 2017 similarly established that for every £1 spent by employers on programmes and activities to support mental health, there was an average return on investment of £5.[5] This suggests that there are compelling business reasons to invest in the wellbeing of employees.

Drivers and detractors of employee wellbeing

It can be difficult to separate individual wellbeing and workplace wellbeing. Issues that might be seen as personal or not work-related, such as bereavement, may well influence wellbeing in the workplace. Similarly, issues at work, such as an excessive workload, might influence how people feel outside of work.

According to the New Economics Foundation, five elements can influence our overall individual wellbeing:

1 Being physically active.
2 Social connections with other people.
3 Taking notice (generally of the good things in our lives).
4 Learning.
5 Giving back to others.

The CIPD has identified several 'domains' of wellbeing, which include several interconnected facets of health and what supports it within the workplace.[6] They suggest these are:

- Health – which includes physical and mental health, as well as having work and a workplace that considers safety. We consider mental health in more detail later.
- Good work – encompassing management, work demands, terms and conditions of employment and the working environment.
- The values and principles of the organization and its leaders – this includes ethical working practices and diversity and inclusion.
- Collective and social elements of work, such as employee voice and good working relationships.
- Opportunities for personal growth and development for employees.
- Facilitating support for good lifestyle choices, such as providing healthy food options.

- Financial wellbeing – supporting employees through fair pay and reward, and general support for financial management.

As you can see, these elements are broad, going beyond simple notions of supporting physical and mental health. They consider the whole person, both in and out of work. This is a useful framework for any organization that wishes to introduce or plan wellbeing strategies and interventions.

In a workplace context, research has identified many factors that influence wellbeing at work. Job-related factors include:

- duties and responsibilities
- the hours of work
- workloads
- the amount of control someone has over how they work
- technology used at work
- job demands and job security
- management

Wellbeing can also be affected negatively by issues like bullying or discrimination.

TIP

Many of these factors can influence wellbeing positively or negatively. For example, if someone has a lot of control over how they work, this is generally good for their wellbeing. If they have very low control over how they do their work, this can negatively influence wellbeing.

Personal factors influence workplace wellbeing, too. Our personal lives, relationship issues, lifestyle and levels of self-esteem can all influence our working lives and our overall wellbeing.

We are all different, and hence even two people undertaking the same work in the same way and at the same organization could experience very different effects on their overall wellbeing. One person might experience stress from a particular job demand, where another might find that demand stretching and interesting. This presents a practical challenge for HR professionals – how do we know what might create wellbeing challenges and how should we best support wellbeing? We will explore some of the answers to these questions in Chapter 6.

Causes of poor wellbeing

As we have seen, some work-related factors have the power to improve wellbeing – or detract from it. In this section, we will briefly consider some potential risk factors for poor wellbeing.

LEADERSHIP AND MANAGEMENT BEHAVIOUR

Leadership and management play a crucial role in shaping workplace culture and influencing employee wellbeing. Leaders are said to have a 'shadow' that they cast over the organizations that they lead, setting the tone and signalling culture. Leaders can, therefore, be powerful role models – for good or for ill. Leaders who demonstrate effective leadership and concern for wellbeing can be a powerful force for good. However, poor management and leadership can cause stress, high workloads and poor working environments.

AUTONOMY AND CONTROL

The level of control an individual has over their work, including when, where and how they work, influences their health and wellbeing. Low levels of control can cause stress; generally providing autonomy and choice is good for wellbeing and employee engagement.

WORKLOAD

High workload is often cited as a reason for mental health-related absence from work. Too much work, too many deadlines, or too few resources, can be stressful or even result in burnout if not addressed long-term. Workloads that are too high also result in other behaviours that can negatively influence health, such as working longer hours or working while on holiday. In turn, these may create physical health issues, as well as stress.

ORGANIZATIONAL CHANGE
Change is an inevitable part of organizational life, but the way it is managed significantly impacts employee wellbeing. Change can be anxiety-inducing, especially if it is not well managed or communicated. Some change programmes may well impact issues like job security, creating further risk around wellbeing, as well as employee engagement.

THE NATURE OF THE WORK
As we noted earlier, every job has demands and particular characteristics, some of which may influence health and wellbeing. Factors such as the working environment, work patterns, and tasks and responsibilities, can all contribute to health and wellbeing. When demands are too great, especially if there is no support in place to address them or if they continue for too long, it may well cause reduced health and wellbeing.

Mental health and stress in the workplace

> **Stress**: An adverse reaction that people have to the pressures placed upon them.

> **Mental health**: An aspect of individual wellbeing that allows people to contribute to society, handle the day-to-day stresses of life and reach their potential.

Work can contribute to good mental health, or it can cause or exacerbate mental health conditions – especially when work is poorly managed or there is too much of it. For many organizations, absence due to poor mental health accounts for a significant amount of their working days lost due to ill health. According to the Health and Safety Executive in the UK, it is the primary reason for absence from work, with conditions like stress, anxiety and depression adding up to more than 16 million working days.[7] In 2020, it was estimated that the total cost to businesses is £42–45 billion per annum, a figure that includes costs relating to turnover, presenteeism and leave.[8]

In 2017, an independent review was undertaken by Lord Dennis Stevenson and Paul Farmer, on behalf of the UK government, into mental health and employers, which became known as the 'Thriving at Work' report.[9] It highlighted the financial cost to the economy of poor mental health, how stigma surrounding mental health can get in the way of open conversations about it, and the potential benefits that can be gained by employers by investing in mental health support. It also recognized how many employees are struggling at work while managing a mental health condition, as well as the number of people that leave their jobs every year as a result.

The report called for employers to adopt a framework for improving mental health, following several core standards. They suggested that if organizations want their employees to thrive at work, they should:

· have a mental health at work plan
· develop mental health awareness among their employees
· encourage conversations about mental health
· monitor employee mental health and wellbeing
· develop effective people managers
· provide good working conditions, including support for personal development and work-life balance

---

STOP AND THINK

Do some research within your organization. Review the core standards for employers as set out by the Thriving at Work report discussed in this chapter.

- Does your organization currently meet the list of core standards?
- Can you identify any gaps or standards that they do not meet?
- Can you identify any areas that need further development?

Disclosure of poor mental health

Not everyone is comfortable telling people they work with that they are experiencing poor mental health. Sometimes, this might be because they have had poor experiences of disclosure in the past and they may not feel safe doing it again. It's not uncommon for people to feel concerned about the stigma that can be associated with mental health conditions or that there might be some sort of negative career impact. The relationship with the employee's line manager can be quite influential in the decision to disclose or not. From the point of view of HR, it is generally better to know if someone is experiencing poor mental health, as this is key to providing the right kind of support or workplace adjustments. While you can encourage people to disclose if they are experiencing poor mental health, this will really only happen if people feel that the organizational culture is sufficiently supportive and safe.

TIP

HR professionals do not need to be experts in mental health to support employees with specific conditions or create an organization in which mental health is supported. It can, however, be useful to understand some basic information about common mental health conditions and their symptoms, and how they may affect someone at work. Look for opportunities to learn more about mental health through further reading, relevant websites, courses or your professional networks.

WHAT WOULD YOU DO?
Number 5

An employee approaches you in confidence and tells you that they are experiencing poor mental health. They tell you they feel anxious, stressed and cannot sleep at night. They do not want to talk to their manager, as they believe they will not be supportive, or it may even harm their promotion prospects.

- What questions could you ask to understand the issue better?
- What advice would you give to the employee?
- How would you respond to their concerns about disclosing their mental health condition?

As well as the information in this chapter, you can undertake further research to help you answer this question. You can learn more about mental health conditions by visiting relevant mental health websites.

Stress

Stress is just one element of mental health at work. It can result in a range of different symptoms for the individual experiencing it, and these, in turn, can lead to organizational outcomes such as reduced productivity, employee turnover, absence from work or even the effectiveness of their thinking and judgement. Over time, high levels of stress can also have a negative influence on physical health.

What makes a role stressful isn't necessarily its seniority or levels of responsibility. As we noted in the previous section, many factors can contribute to or detract from wellbeing at work, and the same is true for what causes stress. The UK Health and Safety Executive (HSE) has identified six areas that can lead to work-related stress called the 'Management Standards'.[10] They are:

1 The demands of the job.
2 Level of control over work.
3 Level of support.
4 Workplace relationships.
5 The role itself.
6 How change is managed.

In Chapter 2, we considered some of the academic theories that apply to employee engagement. Some of these are also relevant to how we think about stress at work. One of these is the theory about 'fit' between the employee and their organization. Imagine, for example, that you passionately believe in sustainability and that we all have a responsibility to conserve the earth's resources, but your employer is wasteful or even, in some way, actively contributes to harming the environment. This could be poor values fit and hence become a source of unhappiness or stress.

We also discussed Job demands-resource theory in Chapter 2. This theory states that every job has its own unique set of demands and resources. Too many demands (such as workload) may lead to negative health outcomes like stress. Resources are those elements of a job that help us or can reduce stress, such as good managerial support, employee autonomy and development opportunities. This theory suggests that if organizations want to reduce stress, they need to focus on reducing demands (where possible) and increasing resources. Resources and demands, however, can also be personal, such as what is going on in an employee's home life, so not all of these will be in the employer's control. This highlights one of the practical challenges for organizations when seeking to support mental health at work – not all of those factors that can support or detract from mental health are work-related. It is, however, important for people professionals, as well as managers and leaders, to have a good understanding of the work activities that influence health and wellbeing.

EXERCISE

Reflect on the roles within your organization, and their duties and responsibilities. Using the six areas contained within the HSE Management Standards, consider whether any roles are more likely to result in stress than others. Think about both the work that's involved and any contextual factors you are aware of. What could you or the organization do to address this?

Measuring wellbeing

Any organization wishing to focus on their employees' wellbeing should carefully consider how to approach it. We will explore different options in Chapter 7. An important activity, whether starting on a wellbeing journey or continuing existing work, is to understand the current state of wellbeing within the workforce. This can help organizations gain important insight, including into potential problem areas that need to be addressed, or areas of potential strengths and good practice.

Wellbeing metrics

Measuring wellbeing can be complex. As we have discussed, wellbeing is subjective, and as work and non-work aspects of life are often integrated, it can be difficult to separate general health issues and work-specific concerns. A range of formal wellbeing measures exist. Some of these relate to general wellbeing, while others are work-specific. Many of the work-specific ones focus on particular areas of wellbeing, such as stress or burnout. These sorts of measurements are usually survey-based. It is not uncommon for organizations to also include some wellbeing-related questions in more general employee surveys, such as the engagement surveys we discussed in Chapter 3. There are other ways to gather useful insights into employee health and wellbeing, and organizations may need to use a range of these to get the bigger picture. For example:

• Data on sickness absence.
• Employee Assistance Programme (EAP) usage (if you have one – we consider these in Chapter 6).
• Occupational Health referrals.
• Internal absence data.

Absence data can include working days lost, reasons for absence or patterns in particular teams or departments. It can be useful to look at the different drivers between short- and long-term absence, as patterns can differ. It is important to remember that not everyone tells the truth about their reasons for absence. For example, if an employee feels it isn't ok for them to say that they are experiencing mental health issues, they may give another reason for their absence from work.

Focus groups or engagement with employee network groups can allow organizations to gather more in-depth information about employee health concerns or needs. These can be useful where there are particular concerns or identified areas for improvement, or to get feedback on activities the organization has undertaken.

Stress risk assessment is another approach that some organizations use. These assessments provide a structured way of assessing the potential risks for work-related stress within an organization, to then be able to address or minimize these risks. A stress risk assessment typically involves:

• identifying any potential risks of stress in the organization generally, and in specific roles
• looking for ways to reduce or remove those risks

- putting a plan in place to reduce the risk of stress and keeping this under regular review.

Mind, a leading mental health charity, recommends that measuring wellbeing should include taking stock of mental health.[11] In addition to some of the measures discussed above, they suggest asking specific questions about stress or mental health in any employee surveys, as well as related questions about the reasonableness of workloads – a known cause of stress at work. For example, you could ask employees to rate on a scale:

- their current general level of wellbeing
- how often they feel stressed at work
- how comfortable they would feel talking to their manager about their wellbeing or mental health

Employees could also be allowed to say what would help them to improve their wellbeing at work.

Understanding the overall wellbeing picture in your organization should guide you on the steps needed to improve and enable wellbeing, as well as reduce risks of poor health. It should be a key starting point for any wellbeing plan or strategy.

EXERCISE

Undertake some research within your organization. Does it currently measure employee wellbeing? If so, what methods are used? See if you can review any of these sources of data.
    Find out the following:

- What are the top three reasons for absence in your organization?
- What percentage of absence from work is related to mental health conditions?
- What is the total 'working days lost' per year statistic – or overall absence percentage?

WHAT WOULD YOU DO?

Number 6

A review of your employee absence data suggests a lot of absences for musculoskeletal reasons (such as neck and back pain). Your data also identifies a lot of short-term absences for minor illnesses like colds and headaches.

- How could you further investigate the causes of musculoskeletal absence?

- Can you identify any interventions the company could introduce to support better musculoskeletal health?

- What advice would you give to managers who have employees taking frequent short-term absences for minor conditions?

You may find it helpful to revisit this question after reading Chapter 8.

Creating the culture for wellbeing

Organizational culture: The unique environment of an organization, encompassing the way people work, how they behave and what they believe and value.

As we saw in our discussions on employee engagement in Chapter 4, every organization has its own culture. Employee wellbeing and organizational culture are linked. Organizational culture shapes the experience an employee has of their work and workplace, and this, in turn, influences their health and wellbeing in many different ways. If a culture is generally a good one, where employees feel that they belong and are included, the management is effective and there are positive workplace relationships, these factors are likely to contribute positively to employees' health. Taking into account some of the stress theories we looked at earlier, employees should feel that there is good fit and balance between resources and demands. Conversely, if there is poor or even toxic workplace culture, this may be deleterious to health.

As we already know, changing organizational culture is not a simple or quick task, and it may be beyond the capabilities of HR professionals alone. There are, however, some actions that HR can lead or support that contribute to creating a culture in which wellbeing is seen as important both for employees and the wider success of the organization. Not every HR department will have all of these in place; in Chapter 7 we will explore how early career HR professionals can influence their organization on health and wellbeing, support manager development and influence buy-in. HR actions to support wellbeing culture include the following:

- A documented wellbeing strategy or policy – while a policy on its own cannot dictate a culture, it sends a signal to employees that the organization cares about their health and wellbeing.
- Train managers – as we explore later in this book, a manager's role in employee wellbeing is highly influential. Their actions contribute to creating a culture that is good for employee wellbeing.
- Communicate the importance of health and wellbeing to employees and managers – talking about wellbeing and being seen to take a proactive stance can help to create a culture that normalizes wellbeing and mental health, therefore enabling people to seek help when they need it.
- The core standards for mental health – as discussed earlier in this chapter, these also contribute to a culture conducive to good wellbeing.

Criticisms of wellbeing at work

Wellbeing washing: Organizations claiming to support health and wellbeing at work, but without necessarily taking it seriously or taking steps to back up this claim.

As already mentioned, not everyone thinks that wellbeing programmes are the right thing to do. Others accept the need for wellbeing but are critical of particular approaches or activities. One criticism about wellbeing programmes is that organizations engage in 'wellbeing washing' – this means that they are implementing wellbeing programmes because it looks good or to improve their reputation, but they are not really committed to it. They might also be engaging in employee wellbeing for cynical aims – such as to get more productivity from the employee, rather than because it is the right thing to do.

As we will see when we explore wellbeing interventions in Chapter 6, many of the activities that organizations typically provide are focused on the employee and helping them to be well or 'cope'. While, on the face of it, this might seem like a good idea, a counterargument is that employees bear all the responsibility for their health, and the organization is not required to change anything that might be contributing to poor health and wellbeing. When organizations offer wellbeing activities, it is generally up to the employee to take part, which means that people who choose not to take part or are aware of the activities are excluded. World-leading expert in wellbeing, Professor Sir Cary Cooper, says that organizations can focus on quick wins like offering simple solutions, such as free fruit or mindfulness, but this will not alone create a culture that prioritizes wellbeing.

Sometimes, health and wellbeing programmes don't always provide what employees really want or need. This might be because organizations opt for what is easy to provide or implement. For example, companies might introduce discounted gym membership when employees would be better served by managers who have been provided with high-quality training on supporting wellbeing at work.

STOP AND THINK

Consider your perspectives on wellbeing at work. List the elements that you believe are essential for a healthy work environment.

If you have ever taken part in any workplace wellbeing activity or event, do you think it helped your wellbeing? Say why, or why not.

EXERCISE

Different employees enjoy different wellbeing activities. While some might enjoy a group exercise class, others might prefer a quiet activity they can do independently.

How can you identify what wellbeing initiatives employees would value? Come up with a list of questions you could ask and identify how you can encourage people to provide feedback.

CHAPTER SUMMARY

- Wellbeing can be defined in many different ways. It incorporates physical and mental health as well as ideas such as work-life balance, burnout and resilience.

- There is an established business case for investing in wellbeing that demonstrates how much organizations can gain from supporting employee health.

- There are many causes of poor health at work, which may or may not be related to the work itself.

- Mental health, including stress, is a significant cause for concern for organizations and can contribute to absence from work. Organizations should have a plan for supporting employee mental health.

- Measuring wellbeing is complex and can be achieved through a range of methods including formal wellbeing measures, absence data and EAP usage, as well as asking questions about stress, mental health and wellbeing in employee surveys.

- Employee wellbeing, like employee engagement, is related to organizational culture. A positive working culture can support good wellbeing.

- Workplace wellbeing initiatives face both barriers to implementation and criticisms; organizations should consider how to address these when developing wellbeing plans and strategies.

REVIEW QUESTIONS

1 Explain why employee wellbeing is important for organizations. How do they benefit from healthy employees?

2 Name one potential organizational risk of poor employee wellbeing.

3 What is stress? Write a definition.

4 Make a list of the different ways organizations can measure employee wellbeing.

Further reading

Mitchell, D (2018) *50 Top Tools for Employee Wellbeing: A complete toolkit for developing happy, healthy, productive and engaged employees*, Kogan Page

Stevenson, D and Farmer, P (2017) Thriving at work: The independent review of mental health and employers, https://assets.publishing. service.gov.uk/media/5a82180e40f0b6230269acdb/thriving-at-work-stevenson-farmer-review.pdf (archived at https://perma.cc/MC6K-E7NH)

Endnotes

1   www.who.int/activities/promoting-well-being (archived at https://perma.cc/QFD3-B5D3).

2   https://neweconomics.org/2008/10/five-ways-to-wellbeing (archived at https://perma.cc/NV7R-CKRJ)

3   www.who.int/data/gho/data/themes/theme-details/GHO/mental-health (archived at https://perma.cc/8LCM-6SM8)

4   https://assets.publishing.service.gov.uk/media/ 5a7c4ae6e5274a2041cf3053/hwwb-dwp-wellness-report-public.pdf (archived at https://perma.cc/56D8-UJWG)

5   www.deloitte.com/uk/en/services/consulting/analysis/mental-health-and-employers-the-case-for-investment.html (archived at https://perma.cc/7Z46-2YJT)

6   www.cipd.org/uk/knowledge/factsheets/well-being-factsheet/ (archived at https://perma.cc/7ZYZ-4HV9)

7   www.hse.gov.uk/statistics/dayslost.htm (archived at https://perma.cc/M2LD-69FW)

8   https://www2.deloitte.com/content/dam/Deloitte/uk/Documents/ public-sector/deloitte-uk-mental-health-employers-monitor-deloitte-oct-2017.pdf

9   www.gov.uk/government/publications/thriving-at-work-a-review-of-mental-health-and-employers (archived at https://perma.cc/87S5-HK4S)

10   www.hse.gov.uk/stress/standards/index.htm (archived at https://perma.cc/224V-XHVM)

11   www.mind.org.uk/media-a/4664/resource_2_take_stock_of_mh_in_ your_workplace_final.pdf (archived at https://perma.cc/YMN2-C2AP)

CHAPTER SIX

Wellbeing strategies and interventions

Introduction

In our last chapter, we considered the meaning of wellbeing at work, why it matters and what supports and detracts from it. This chapter discusses wellbeing in practice. We look at what organizations can do to support wellbeing at work, both at a strategic level and a practical, day-to-day one.

We consider the activities, initiatives and programmes that employers can undertake to support wellbeing at work, and, taking into account all the relevant evidence, how you can decide which ones are best suited to your organization. Finally, we explore how to communicate wellbeing initiatives and encourage employees to take part, identifying potential barriers that might get in the way, and how to measure the impact of your wellbeing activity. This chapter lays the groundwork for Chapters 7 and 8, which consider HR's role in wellbeing in practice and how HR can support managers to contribute to engagement and wellbeing.

LEARNING OBJECTIVES

By the end of this chapter, you will be able to:

*   Define wellbeing strategy.
*   Explain the term 'wellbeing intervention'.
*   Identify the main wellbeing interventions offered by employers and their potential benefits.
*   Understand the importance of seeking out the evidence base for interventions.
*   Explain how to determine the right interventions for your organization.
*   Explain how to engage employees with interventions.
*   Measure the impact of interventions.

What is a wellbeing strategy?

Wellbeing strategy: A formal plan that sets out how an organization aims to support the health and wellbeing of its omployees.

A wellbeing strategy is simply a plan that sets out the organization's approach to supporting the health and wellbeing of its employees. Typically, it is set out in a document or formal policy. Wellbeing strategies vary but typically include some overall goals for health and wellbeing, accompanied by objectives and an action plan. Ideally, wellbeing strategies align to broader organizational strategies so it's clear to employees and managers how employee wellbeing contributes to supporting these goals.

A holistic strategy does not focus on just one aspect of wellbeing, but recognizes the interconnectedness of different aspects of health, and the whole person, at work and outside of work. Such strategies will address physical and mental health, and possibly some wider concepts such as digital or financial wellbeing. Effective wellbeing strategies focus on creating a whole organizational environment in which employees can be well, engaged and satisfied at work. On a practical level, strategies might also list the wellbeing interventions that the organization provides. A good wellbeing strategy should have:

- a clear goal or vision for employee wellbeing within the organization
- objectives that will help to support the goal
- a defined set of actions or steps, ideally with an accompanying timeline
- identification of resources that will enable implementation
- a plan for engagement and communication
- a set of measures upon which the programme and its outcomes can be assessed

What is a wellbeing intervention?

Wellbeing intervention: An activity undertaken by an organization to support employee wellbeing in the workplace.

Wellbeing interventions are the activities that organizations undertake to support employee wellbeing in the workplace. They aim to result in change – either for the individual or within the organization. Interventions operate at a variety of levels and vary from strategic to everyday. In their book on work psychology, Arnold et al (2020) distinguish between three types of intervention – primary, secondary and tertiary.[1]

Primary interventions

Primary interventions are activities that seek to tackle the sources of wellbeing problems at work and, wherever possible, prevent them from arising. An example of a primary wellbeing intervention would be identifying the potential demands of a job and then designing (or redesigning) its duties and responsibilities in such a way that it minimizes the potential for stress. Another example would be providing detailed development for people managers so that they may lead and manage in such a way that does not cause stressors for their teams.

Secondary interventions

Secondary interventions are those activities that help employees maintain their wellbeing at work or help them cope with wellbeing challenges. These might include wellbeing promotion or activities. At this level, while these activities might be useful for the individual, there is no real attempt to change any causes of poor wellbeing or the workplace itself. They place the responsibility on the employee to be responsible for their own wellbeing and to deal with any challenges they experience as a result of their work.

Tertiary interventions

Finally, tertiary interventions are activities that provide support for those who are already ill, such as occupational health or return to work support after an absence from work.

A successful approach to organizational wellbeing will ensure that there are wellbeing interventions taking place at every level. A common criticism of wellbeing interventions is that organizations focus too much on secondary and tertiary activities because they are the easiest to do. Primary interventions are more difficult to identify and implement.

Many different recommendations suggest how employers can go about supporting wellbeing at work, which can make it difficult to know what to do in practice. Some of the activities put in place by organizations do not have a strong evidence base, and, as we saw in Chapter 5, another criticism is that workplace wellbeing programmes are 'tokenistic', or that they fail to tackle the real sources of poor wellbeing. We will address some of the challenges later in this chapter.

TIP

Does your organization have a formal wellbeing strategy or policy? If it does, review any relevant documents and consider whether they include clear goals, action plans and measurable outcomes for wellbeing. Identify who has overall responsibility for delivering your wellbeing strategy.

Common wellbeing interventions

Organizations provide a range of wellbeing interventions and activities. Here are just a few of the most common.

Wellbeing promotion and awareness

Many organizations have general programmes and activities to promote wellbeing in general, and in work. These programmes vary from organization to organization, but they often include activities, challenges or awareness days focusing on particular aspects of health. Promotion may provide information or encourage general health and wellbeing.

Policies

Some organizations have policies and procedures that set out their approach to supporting wellbeing. These could be general or focus on specific issues, such as stress at work or setting up safe workstations for ergonomics and screen health. These policies normally set out the roles and responsibilities of the wider organization, managers and employees themselves.

Employee assistance programmes (EAPs)

EAPs are designed to provide confidential support to employees on a range of issues, often involving some aspect of mental health. They can provide employees with access to guidance and sources of information, and often include the provision of one-to-one counselling.

Mental Health First Aid (MHFA)

Mental Health First Aid is a formal accreditation, undertaken by employees and supported by their organization, which trains people on supporting employees with mental health difficulties. Mental health first aiders provide signposting only; this is not an advisory role.

Mindfulness and meditation

Some organizations encourage employees to engage with mindfulness or meditation techniques to support their mental health and aid relaxation. This can either be provided through events and workshops or via apps.

Workshops and training

Sometimes part of wellbeing promotion activities or events, workshops or training often address specific health issues such as stress management, mental health awareness, nutrition, physical fitness, work-life balance, digital wellbeing or menopause.

Physical health support

Gym membership and Cycle to Work schemes are typical examples of physical health support interventions. Some organizations also offer exercise classes or support for healthy eating and hydration. Sometimes, these interventions are aligned with a particular work-related health risk, such as musculoskeletal issues from driving or lifting.

Manager training

Many organizations offer some form of training or development to people managers on the subject of workplace health. This might range from the practical (supporting employees with a safe workstation setup) to more holistic ways of supporting employees to be healthy while at work.

Health checks

Employee health checks can take several forms, from providing a full health screening to providing checks for a particular health condition, such as a diabetes, healthy heart or cholesterol check.

Healthcare cash plan

These schemes, which can be funded in a range of different ways by employers, allow employees to claim back the costs of certain medical treatments or routine health costs such as dental work, optical care or physiotherapy.

Occupational health

Occupational health services can fulfil a range of functions. These include advising employers on an individual's fitness to work, such as after a period of ill-health or absence. They may undertake health assessments necessary for the role or advise employers on reasonable adjustments in the workplace to support disabled employees. Large organizations may have an in-house function but others may use outsourced, specialist providers.

Wellbeing champions

These are typically employee champions, who usually receive some specific training. They are advocates for employee wellbeing in their organizations and may organize or promote wellbeing activities.

Financial wellbeing

Typically, this involves helping people manage their finances and can include vehicles to help people save, or information on certain financial stages, such as retirement planning. It may also include supporting employees experiencing financial difficulties through debt advice services.

Support and policies for specific employee groups

Some organizations create policies that support specific employee groups, such as parents, carers or disabled employees. They may also set up support or networking groups, often for employees with a particular characteristic that may influence health or who have a wellbeing condition. This might include a disabled employees' group, a menopause group or a cancer network.

Other interventions

There are other programmes, policies and activities that organizations offer to employees to support employee health and wellbeing, but these may not necessarily be considered a formal wellbeing intervention. These might include:

- the provision of flexible working arrangements
- reward and recognition
- provision of development opportunities
- ergonomic provision, such as consideration of furniture or the working environment
- general leadership and management training and development
- initiatives to improve employee engagement or organizational culture

The wellbeing interventions offered by organizations may be influenced by budget, available resources, the needs of the workforce and the work that they do, and the organization's culture.

> **EXERCISE**
>
> What wellbeing interventions does your organization currently offer to its employees? Are they primary, secondary or tertiary? Identify if you have any gaps in your levels of provision.

The evidence for interventions

The evidence for wellbeing interventions is lacking and sometimes result in mixed findings. This presents a practical challenge for HR professionals. Academic studies in this area typically review the extent to which any particular intervention, such as the ones discussed earlier in this chapter, makes a measurable difference to employee health and wellbeing. As we have already seen, workplace wellbeing can be difficult to measure. It is influenced by both work and non-work factors, and it can be challenging to differentiate between short-term and long-term health effects.

One study into the outcomes of workplace wellbeing interventions found that employees who took part in individual interventions, such as relaxation classes and using wellbeing apps, have the same mental wellbeing as those who did not.[2] Mental Health First Aid has been found to lack a reliable evidence base.[3] In contrast, other studies have found that particular interventions do work. Providing counselling, promoting increased movement and standing at work, promoting wellbeing, job design and training managers have been found, in some studies, to support employee health and wellbeing. However, some of these studies were undertaken in particular workplaces, and it can be difficult to know if results will be replicated in a different organization that has a different context, job roles or culture.

When introducing a new wellbeing intervention, or reviewing an existing one, it is important to look at the evidence base. This will contribute to effective, informed decision-making and allow HR professionals to add value by providing sound advice to leaders or managers. It is also important, however, to look wider than the evidence base and consider how the intervention under consideration will work in your organization, as well as any relevant internal data.

EXERCISE

Identify one intervention undertaken by your organization. Research its evidence base, considering both academic sources and industry reports.

• Does the intervention have a strong evidence base?

• Can you compare this to any of your internal data to determine if it is a 'good' intervention to offer?

As well as research into specific interventions, other relevant evidence might be useful, especially when deciding on interventions, which we will discuss next. In Chapter 5, we looked at research from the CIPD and the UK Health and Safety Executive. These organizations highlight:

• the significant impact of people managers and their management skills on employee wellbeing
• the detrimental effect of poorly managed or communicated organizational change
• the need for wellbeing programmes and strategies to tackle a range of different aspects of health
• the scale of mental health-related absence from work and its associated costs
• that the culture of the organization, as well as working conditions, directly influence employee health

It is, therefore, important for interventions to be construed broadly and go beyond offering the kinds of activities, events and initiatives listed earlier in this chapter. Whether this is realistic or achievable will depend on the organization, the attitudes of leaders and the maturity of its approach to wellbeing. HR professionals can play an important role in influencing ideas about wellbeing, which we explore in depth in Chapters 7 and 8.

The research from the CIPD, HSE and Thrive reports suggest that the following interventions should provide a wellbeing benefit to organizations:

- Manager and leader training on their role in supporting health and wellbeing – including how their day-to-day management can influence employee health.
- A consideration for wellbeing during organizational change, including, where appropriate, targeted supporting wellbeing activities.
- A focus on mental health in any workplace wellbeing programme, including targeted wellbeing interventions.
- Aligning any culture change activities with wellbeing initiatives and ensuring that wellbeing interventions do not only focus on secondary and tertiary initiatives but incorporate activities at the critical primary level.

Deciding on interventions

As we have seen, there are many different interventions, approaches and strategies available to organizations to support health and wellbeing at work. Any organization will likely need to undertake a variety of different approaches if they want to truly make a difference to employee wellbeing.

The best interventions will be the ones that are most suited to the specific organization, addressing the potential wellbeing risks and challenges within that organization and the kind of work that it does. A tailored approach should lead to the most positive outcomes. The most effective interventions will also consider both employee interventions and organizational ones.

Organizations should not necessarily seek to offer every wellbeing intervention that they can – but at the same time, they need to offer a range. This balancing act can be difficult for HR professionals.

There is no single intervention that will support wellbeing at work, nor one single 'best' approach. Given people's differences and wide range of needs, providing several interventions (which may be interconnected and mutually supporting) is a good approach. As mentioned earlier, where possible, interventions should be primary, secondary and tertiary in nature.

An important first step is to understand the current state of wellbeing within the workforce by measuring it. We covered this in Chapter 5. Use the insight to guide you when determining necessary interventions, focusing specifically on the following:

- What does your absence data tell you? Absence data, especially the reasons why people take time off work, should be a key driver of decisions about wellbeing interventions. For example, if work-related stress is often cited as a reason for work-related absence, it would be appropriate to introduce interventions that tackle the causes of stress as well as support employees experiencing it. Check for patterns in teams and departments, and any differences between long- and short-term absences.
- Engage with employees. Employees themselves are a valuable source of information to guide you on what interventions will help them and their specific needs, so be sure to include the employee voice in your decision-making process. You can engage with employee network groups if you have them, such as disabled staff or working parents' networks. You could also create a group of Wellbeing Champions to provide feedback.

- Check in with your EAP provider if you have one. They can provide you with information on the kinds of issues that employees contact them about, or any important trends.
- Look at exit data. Exit data is another good source of information on health and wellbeing at work. Some employees experiencing work-related issues that are affecting their health may simply choose to leave. Exit interviews can be a useful way to surface this sort of information.
- Check what has been tried before. Consider what activities may have taken place in the past and how these were received by employees and their managers.
- Talk to managers. As we explore in Chapter 8, managers have practical responsibilities concerning employee health and wellbeing, especially when absence from work is involved, or when employees have long-term health conditions that require support or workplace adjustments. Talking to managers about their experiences and needs may also surface useful information to guide your decision-making.
- Consider the diversity of your workforce as well as the roles that they do. For example, employees who spend all day on screens may benefit from digital wellbeing interventions. Certain demographics may be more susceptible to specific health conditions, such as diabetes or poor heart health, and might benefit from interventions to meet these needs.
- Reflect on your culture and consider the causes of poor wellbeing and any barriers to workplace wellbeing (discussed in Chapter 5). Consider what risks you may have in your workplace and which interventions might address them. Refer to the section on 'measuring wellbeing' in Chapter 5 for information on stress risk assessments.

If an external provider is supplying a wellbeing intervention, ask them for evidence or research on the efficacy of their products or services. What benefits have they been able to verify? What outcomes have other customers identified? What feedback have they received from other customers?

When a wellbeing intervention is implemented, it is important to capture your data on how useful it is; we consider how to do this later in the chapter.

EXERCISE

Based on the discussions in this chapter so far, are there any wellbeing interventions that your organization does not offer, that you think they should? Undertake some internal research if necessary.

If you can identify any interventions that are not currently provided, how would they benefit your employees? What would you need to do to make a recommendation to your organization?

Mental health interventions

Given the extent to which poor mental health influences attendance at work, many organizations might wish to consider at least some interventions that are specific to mental health, either to support employees who are experiencing symptoms or to prevent them from arising in the first place.

Mind, the mental health charity, suggests several questions for organizations to consider when thinking about how to support mental health at work.[4] These are:

- Is there awareness of mental health at all levels in your organization?
- Do you have clear policies for managing mental health at work?
- Are your managers trained in mental health, and confident to converse with employees? Are they properly equipped to support employees who are experiencing mental health problems?
- Do you know how many of your employees experience poor mental health? Would your employees feel confident that they can disclose a mental health condition to you?

Reflecting on these questions and their answers may help identify gaps and appropriate wellbeing interventions to support mental health in the workplace.

Engaging employees with wellbeing interventions

Employee participation in and engagement with wellbeing interventions is, of course, crucial to the success of workplace wellbeing initiatives. There can be barriers to participating, as we shall discuss shortly.

To encourage participation in wellbeing interventions, organizations can try some of the following:

- Tailor interventions to the needs of the workforce. You can potentially establish these from your knowledge of roles or workforce data, such as absence records or employee engagement surveys. You can complement this by simply asking people what they would find beneficial.
- Regular promotion of activities and options. Employees may need regular prompts and reminders about what wellbeing opportunities are available. This will help keep the offering at the top of employees' minds, which is especially important if they begin to experience ill health.
- Leadership involvement and role modelling. When leaders engage with wellbeing programmes or specific interventions, they send a signal to employees that this is an acceptable use of time, and that wellbeing is important. It can permit employees to engage – contributing to a supportive organizational culture.
- Create a broad wellbeing offering. Different employees will have different wellbeing needs. Accordingly, any wellbeing programme should be as broad as possible within the circumstances and budget available, addressing different aspects of health (such as those set out by the CIPD, discussed in Chapter 5).

- Work with Wellbeing Champions. As we noted in Chapter 5, some organizations set up teams of champions who are interested in wellbeing. These individuals can be a valuable way to communicate and encourage participation, especially if they can talk about the potential benefits of activities.
- Introduce competition or gamification. Some employees may be motivated by a wellbeing challenge. For example, introduce a steps challenge that can be undertaken across teams or fund some places at a sporting event. Participation in challenges and competitions should always be voluntary.
- Communicate impact and benefits. Use communication channels to share success stories or testimonials and highlight recent events. This can help to reinforce the value of participation.

TIP

Check out how your organization currently promotes its wellbeing activities and events. Can you identify any opportunities for improvement and development that you could share with the relevant owner? Consider how you could effectively propose new solutions.

Barriers to workplace wellbeing

There can be several barriers to workplace wellbeing and employee participation in activities. There may be a lack of leadership buy-in and support, or cynicism or lack of awareness about the benefits of wellbeing activity. Sometimes, employees just do not want to engage with the idea of wellbeing at all, or wellbeing at work in particular, preferring to separate what they see as their work and non-work parts of their life. As we discussed in the section on mental health earlier in this chapter, culture might also be a barrier, with employees not feeling that it is ok to say that they need support for health and wellbeing, especially mental health. Part of any good workplace wellbeing approach should consider what barriers might exist, and how these can be overcome. Other potential barriers include the following:

- One-size-fits all approach – organizations cannot address every potential health and wellbeing issue that may arise within their workforce, so sometimes generic solutions are the only option. These might not meet everyone's needs, especially diverse groups.
- Mental health stigma – as we have already discussed, mental health stigma does persist, and some employees may not feel that they can come forward to seek support at work.
- Confidentiality concerns – some employees may be concerned about engaging with workplace wellbeing initiatives, especially if they have a sensitive health condition, or one that, as noted above, can be subject to stigma.
- Workload – some employees may feel that they just do not have the time to engage with workplace wellbeing initiatives or focus on their own health.

Some employees may be hesitant to take part in activities due to time constraints, lack of awareness, or concerns about privacy and stigma. This may be influenced by role; for example, managers may not feel comfortable attending a workshop about stress with their team. If wellbeing activities are not seen as relevant to employees' specific needs and interests, they may not feel motivated to participate. Employees may also be influenced by their manager; if the manager does not actively encourage participation, employees may not feel that it is considered a good use of their work time.

Identifying your own potential barriers to participation can act as a key to addressing them. This may need to be undertaken at an intervention-by-intervention level. For example, if you offer stress awareness workshops, what are the potential barriers to employees participating? The exercise below will help you to work through this process.

EXERCISE

Identify one wellbeing intervention that your organization offers. What barriers might be associated with it that may impact employee engagement with this intervention? Use some of the points below to guide your thinking:

- Reflect on your different employee groups. Are there differences between how employees or managers might feel about participating in the activity? Are there any other groups that might have barriers unique to them that will get in the way?

- Consider accessibility. Can everyone participate equally in the intervention? Is anyone excluded?

- When and where is the intervention taking place? Are there any factors about the location and timing that might influence engagement? Are there any employees who cannot participate because of timing and/or location?

- Could employees feel concerned about stigma or confidentiality? Are there any reasons for this belief?

- Understanding of the intervention and the benefits. Are the potential benefits of engaging with the intervention understood? Is the actual intervention clearly communicated? For example, if your intervention is an EAP, do employees understand what that is and how they can use it?

- Are there any aspects of your specific organizational culture that may influence attendance or participation?

Measuring the impact of your interventions

It is important to understand if wellbeing interventions are having a positive impact on wellbeing or 'working'. Of course, first of all, it is necessary to understand what we mean by impact. Maybe your organization wants to see a reduction in absence levels, the reduction of a particular type of absence (such as stress), or they may want to see an improvement in knowledge about health or employee wellness overall. It is a good idea to know what you want out of interventions before you implement them.

There are several ways that organizations can measure the impact of their wellbeing interventions. One of these is overall engagement and take-up. You could look at the following:

- The participation levels with each intervention. How many people attend a particular workshop or use your EAP service, for example? Remember that while this might indicate the level of appetite for a particular intervention, it does not tell you whether or not it makes an actual difference to someone's health and wellbeing.
- Feedback on specific interventions. Asking employees how useful they found interventions can be insightful, but it won't necessarily tell you whether they are supporting health or leading to long-term positive health outcomes. Participants may find interventions interesting or enjoyable, but they may not act on the information they're given.

Employee surveys provide a good opportunity to seek information on overall satisfaction with wellbeing programmes and initiatives. If your organization has an employee survey, and it doesn't include questions related to wellbeing interventions, you could consider adding some. For example:

- Have you ever used one of our wellbeing services or attended a wellbeing event?
- How would you rate our wellbeing events and activities?

- What would you like us to include in future wellbeing activities?

Wellbeing activities and programmes can be forgotten over time if they are not regularly promoted. It's common for employees to engage with interventions when they are first launched, but for interest to wane over time. It's therefore useful to periodically check that employees know about the interventions on offer. This is particularly true for EAPs where regular communication of their benefits is said to be important in ensuring ongoing use.

TIP

Use employee surveys (either general surveys or those specific to wellbeing) to promote activities and interventions and understand awareness levels. List everything on offer and ask respondents to say whether or not they are aware of each one.

Over the longer term, wellbeing data (such as absence data) may indicate whether a particular intervention is successful. Indicators such as overall absence levels or reasons for absence can give clues about whether activities are having the desired effect. It is, however, difficult to truly identify causation as behavioural changes may take time to manifest, and external factors could also influence the data. You can review absence data to check the following:

- Are overall absence levels changing?
- Are particular reasons for absence changing?
- What differences can you identify between teams and departments? Are there any notable differences concerning absence levels and reasons for absence?
- How long are people off for – is absence short- or long-term – and what changes can you observe over time?

> **TIP**
>
> Always measure the impact of your wellbeing interventions.
> Consider take-up levels and feedback. Check which are your most
> popular interventions and think about what this tells you about
> the needs of your workforce.

In Chapter 5, we considered the importance of organizational culture and how this can influence employee health and wellbeing. This discussion is also relevant to interventions. An organization can offer any range of wellbeing interventions, follow all so-called best practice and spend significant sums of money on implementation, but if the culture is poor or problematic, these interventions will probably not make a positive, long-term impact on employee wellbeing. Even worse, employees might become disillusioned. They might recognize that the culture is poor, but you are only making token gestures to change it.

> **STOP AND THINK**
>
> Reflect on your learning about wellbeing so far.
> - Has anything challenged your previous views on employee wellbeing?
> - What has been the most interesting or useful thing you have learned?

CHAPTER SUMMARY
- A wellbeing strategy is an organization's formal plan for supporting employee health and wellbeing.
- Wellbeing interventions are the activities that an organization undertakes intending to support health and wellbeing, and are usually part of the strategy.

- Numerous wellbeing interventions exist, which can be broadly categorized as primary, secondary and tertiary.

- The evidence base for some interventions is mixed – not all interventions make a measurable impact on employee health and wellbeing.

- No single set of interventions can support health and wellbeing in all organizations – this depends on factors such as the work, culture and industry. Organizations need to determine the most appropriate interventions for their context.

- It is not enough to simply introduce interventions. Organizations and HR professionals must work to promote them and the value of participating in them to employees.

- There is little point in introducing interventions if you can't measure their impact. Decide what you want each intervention to achieve and determine the right metrics to measure success.

REVIEW QUESTIONS

1 Explain the difference between a wellbeing strategy and a wellbeing intervention.

2 How can you measure the impact of wellbeing interventions so that HR can know 'what works'? Suggest at least two different options.

3 Make a list of common wellbeing interventions.

Further reading

Stevenson, D and Farmer, P (2017) Thriving at work: The independent review of mental health and employers, https://assets.publishing. service.gov.uk/media/5a82180e40f0b6230269acdb/thriving-at-work-stevenson-farmer-review.pdf (archived at https://perma.cc/MC6K-E7NH)

Mitchell, D (2018) *50 Top Tools for Employee Wellbeing: A complete toolkit for developing happy, healthy, productive and engaged employees*, Kogan Page

Endnotes

1 Randall, R, Coyne, I, Patterson, F and Arnold, J (2020) *Work Psychology: Understanding human behaviour in the workplace*, Pearson Higher Ed
2 https://onlinelibrary.wiley.com/doi/full/10.1111/irj.12418 (archived at https://perma.cc/L8H3-KFDA)
3 https://www.cochranelibrary.com/cdsr/doi/10.1002/14651858. CD013127.pub2/full (archived at https://perma.cc/RNR9-5FBR)
4 https://www.mind.org.uk/media-a/4664/resource_2_take_stock_of_ mh_in_your_workplace_final.pdf (archived at https://perma.cc/ YMN2-C2AP)

CHAPTER SEVEN

HR's role in engagement and wellbeing

Introduction

In this chapter, we discuss HR's role in engagement and wellbeing and consider some practical activities that early career HR professionals should understand and be confident and competent to undertake. We distinguish between the roles and responsibilities of HR professionals and the roles of people managers, including how to work effectively with managers on these important topics. This chapter has a practical focus and advises early career HR professionals on topics such as managing boundaries, getting buy-in for engagement and wellbeing initiatives and balancing the needs of employees and the organization.

We look at employee engagement through the lens of the employment lifecycle, considering how day-to-day HR activities from recruitment to exit can influence the employee experience and therefore how employees feel about their work and the organization they work for. We also view wellbeing through a practical lens and look at how to support employees who are unwell or need workplace support.

LEARNING OBJECTIVES

By the end of this chapter, you will be able to:

• Explain the role of HR in supporting employee engagement and wellbeing.

• Discuss the importance of working effectively with managers on engagement and wellbeing.

• Understand how to balance responsibilities to the organization with responsibilities to employees.

• Describe activities that early career HR professionals can undertake to support engagement.

• Describe activities that early career HR professionals can undertake to support wellbeing.

HR's role in engagement and wellbeing

The HR role is a varied one, and exactly what responsibilities fall within it differ from organization to organization. HR professionals may be specialists and focus on one particular aspect of HR work. Others might be generalists involved in anything to do with people at work. HR professionals might be part of a large team or have sole responsibility for the function. This chapter, therefore, considers general principles while recognizing that there is no single 'best' way to do HR, and that the demands and responsibilities differ depending on the roles, industry and context and should reflect the needs of the organization. This chapter, along with Chapter 8, suggests practical options for HR professionals to support engagement and wellbeing.

The maturity of the organization from an HR perspective and the overall skill level of managers also influences the day-to-day work of HR professionals. For example, if HR is a relatively new function in a small organization, or if managers are relatively new to managing, the HR practitioner may need to take a very different approach to one they might take in an organization with a more developed understanding of the importance of HR.

Generally, the responsibility for employee engagement and wellbeing sits within the organization as a whole and its senior leaders. It is not the sole responsibility of HR to ensure that employees are well, happy and engaged – this would be impossible to achieve as engagement and wellbeing are heavily influenced by the culture of the organization and its managers. HR may, however, have formal ownership over many of the related policies, suppliers and processes. It will also typically have responsibility for the employee lifecycle, points of which are also highly influential in the employee's overall experience of work and their organization, as we shall explore.

The role of HR can be thought of as one of supporting, enabling and advising. HR professionals should understand these subjects and be able to provide specialist advice and guidance on how an organization can work towards an engaged and healthy workforce. The following lists, which may differ depending on context, indicates what should ideally be HR's responsibility, and what should be the managers' responsibility, regarding engagement and wellbeing. We explore the role of managers in more depth in Chapter 8. The role of HR professionals in engagement and wellbeing is to:

- provide advice on creating a culture in which engagement and wellbeing can thrive
- create relevant policies and processes, especially throughout the employee lifecycle
- support managers to develop the skills, behaviours and experience to be good managers, enable wellbeing and drive engagement
- offer specialist advice when issues arise within the organization concerning engagement and wellbeing

A lot of activity relating to people within organizations is delivered by managers, even if HR 'owns' the process or policy. The role of managers in engagement and wellbeing is to:

- develop their understanding of wellbeing and engagement at work, and how their day-to-day activities as managers can influence these
- manage in a way that is conducive to supporting engagement and wellbeing within their teams
- help to create a culture of engagement and wellbeing within their areas of responsibility
- act on specific issues that arise within their teams – with the support of HR when they need it
- address practical issues, especially relating to wellbeing and health, using the organization's policies and procedures

Working with managers on engagement and wellbeing

The work of HR is done with and through people managers. At all stages of an HR career, managers are key stakeholders. Establishing effective working relationships between HR and managers is, therefore, an important part of the HR role. This is true of lifecycle activity (which, as we have discussed, has a key influence on engagement) and in broader projects and initiatives.

The most effective working relationships between HR and managers are characterized by collaboration, mutual trust, respect and an understanding of each other's priorities. Strong relationships also pave the way for new HR initiatives and programmes.

Relationships flourish when HR professionals align their engagement and wellbeing activities with the needs of the organization, seek to understand managers' day-to-day challenges, and provide quality and timely support and advice. Good people practices (especially those within the employee lifecycle, discussed later) should empower managers in their work and to be the best managers that they can be. HR departments that act in a silo, fail to respond quickly or act as more of a policing or directive function, are not likely to become trusted partners.

We will now explore some of the challenges that can arise when working with managers and how to overcome them. In the next chapter, we will consider this subject further, discussing how to help managers become good at the people aspects of their role.

Managing boundaries

It is important for HR professionals at all levels, but especially early career HR professionals, to set and maintain appropriate boundaries between themselves and employees and themselves and managers.

When supporting employees, especially when supporting them through difficult situations or personal circumstances, it can be easy to allow boundaries to become blurred. HR professionals must always be clear not to go beyond their professional role; they should provide information and options but should refrain from offering advice, especially if that advice falls outside the scope of their role. For example, if an employee appears to be experiencing mental health difficulties, it would be appropriate for an HR professional to signpost sources of specialist support or provide information on related company policies. It would not be appropriate to offer personal support or advice on what the employee should do.

Similarly, you may need to be clear with people managers about what should fall under their responsibility and what should fall under HR's. As we discussed earlier, these responsibilities may vary depending on the organization, policies and the skill level of the manager. It is not uncommon for responsibilities to become blurred. Managers may feel that HR should undertake some of the people aspects of their role, whereas HR may think that these tasks should be undertaken by the manager.

The tips below can help you manage this potentially tricky issue. If you do not feel that you can directly influence these yourself, consider talking to your manager or making relevant suggestions for improvement.

- Any related HR policies and procedures should ideally include a section that sets out HR's and managers' responsibilities for implementation. Check your policies and flag with your manager if this information is unclear.
- Discuss responsibilities for specific tasks and key result areas related to activities and projects in advance.
- Provide training for managers so they can fulfil their responsibilities while using HR for additional support and advice.
- If managers request that HR undertake tasks which should more properly be conducted by themselves, do not be afraid to professionally push back and highlight why they are a managerial responsibility.

HR departments mustn't become a function that deals with difficult conversations, delivering bad news or handling conflict. Not only is this not the role of a good, value-adding HR department, but it also prevents managers from developing good management and leadership skills. Instead, HR professionals should support and guide managers in addressing these challenges directly, providing training where necessary. This will help to build long-term, collaborative relationships between managers and HR.

WHAT WOULD YOU DO?
Number 7

A manager tells you that they think the HR team should be responsible for managing absence from work and asks you to meet with several employees from their team to discuss reasons for their recent absences and advise them about company absence standards.

- Would you agree to this request?
- Why, or why not?
- If you do not think you should agree to this request, what would you say to the manager?

Use the information in the 'managing boundaries' section to help you with this question.

Getting buy-in for initiatives

Many initiatives that relate to employee engagement or employee health and wellbeing require investment in time or resources (typically a financial investment). HR professionals who want to seek support or investment for new engagement or wellbeing plans may need to present a rationale or a business case to formally gain the necessary approvals.

Many businesses recognize the benefits of investing in engagement or wellbeing, but specific activities may need to be costed and a return on investment demonstrated. Senior leaders are often the key stakeholders who can agree to such proposals and show their support for them to the wider organization and other managers.

If you want to propose new activities or initiatives on engagement and wellbeing, here are some key considerations and areas to include:

- Explain clearly what you are proposing and why you think it is important. What problem will be solved by the proposal, or what new benefits or opportunities will it deliver to the organization?
- Collate relevant internal HR data. Examples could include previous engagement scores or survey data, absence data, turnover, recruitment and turnover figures or demographic

data on employees (this is especially relevant when considering any impact of activities on diversity). You can include both qualitative and quantitative data sources.

- Review relevant evidence from external sources. As discussed in our section on evidence-based decision-making in Chapter 2, this might include data from academic research, management consultancies or relevant professional bodies.
- Detail the costs and expected benefits of your plan, including any expected return on investment. Examples of return on investment for HR initiatives can include cost savings, reduced turnover, reduced absenteeism or increased productivity. There may also be less tangible benefits, such as improved employer brand – these are harder to quantify but should still be mentioned in a business case.
- Set out the decision you are asking leaders or stakeholders to make – what are you asking for? If there is more than one option or an alternative to your proposal, say so, but make a final clear and supported recommendation.
- Good business cases include an implementation plan with a timeline, key milestones and information on how the success or outcomes of the activities will be reviewed and assessed. Highlight any risks or challenges that you have identified and how these will be addressed in the implementation.

Following these tips will help to ensure a business case is successful. Be sure to consider likely challenges or questions you might receive and how you will address these. Preparation supports success!

Balancing the organization and its employees

HR professionals need to balance responsibilities to the organization with responsibilities to employees and navigate the differing expectations that can arise. For example, employees might feel that HR professionals are there to help them resolve their problems or issues at work. In addition to the challenges discussed in the previous section, where managers may feel that HR should do some of their 'people' tasks, employees can have similar misconstrued ideas about what HR should do or does in practice. This miscommunication can be especially problematic if employees are experiencing health and wellbeing issues such as stress – they may want their HR representative to intervene and take steps to resolve this stress for them. As we have seen, this is not the true role of HR. However, in some organizations HR has historically had a 'welfare' basis, and occasionally some HR professionals may take more of an interventionist role, especially around health, depending on what is needed or expected within a given organization.

Ultimately, HR is employed by an organization to deliver its people strategies and practices to help the organization achieve its objectives. Some people, however, can think that HR is there to support employees or act as a sort of arbitrator or mediator between them and the organization, especially if the employee is, for some reason, unhappy or unsatisfied.

In the same way that it is important to manage expectations of the role of HR with people managers, it is important to manage them with employees to avoid unrealistic expectations or even damaging relationships. Bear these tips in mind:

- When an employee comes to you for help, be clear about what you can and cannot do within your role. Do not over-promise.
- If an employee asks you to do something – such as speak to a manager on their behalf about a problem they have had – you do not necessarily have to agree if it does not feel like the right approach. Say so and explain why. To avoid this issue arising in the first place, introduce the purpose and scope of HR's role to employees during onboarding to set realistic expectations.

- Encourage employees, with your guidance and support, to take ownership of their issues or concerns by offering resources or explaining options.
- If appropriate, facilitate a conversation between the employee and their manager to resolve issues directly, rather than intervening on the employee's behalf.

If this is an ongoing issue in your organization, it may be necessary to re-set expectations, including at a senior level. Engage your manager for support – it is a challenge they are likely to have faced themselves in their career at some point.

Supporting employee engagement in practice

As we have already discussed, there are many different roles that HR professionals may play relating to employee engagement. Depending on your role and responsibilities these might include:

- managing employee feedback processes, such as administering or analysing employee engagement surveys or undertaking exit interviews
- advising managers on employee engagement and employee experience, supporting them in their role within this topic
- managing relevant suppliers, such as employee engagement survey providers
- supporting the development or implementation of employee engagement action plans after receiving employee feedback
- undertaking activities across the employee lifecycle that support or improve engagement – discussed below
- implementing initiatives designed to improve employee engagement – such as some of those discussed in Chapter 4

EXERCISE

Review the list of roles and responsibilities in the previous list. Which of these activities, if any, are present in your current role? Can you identify any opportunities to gain further experience or knowledge in areas within which you are not currently involved? Consider how you can address any skills gaps. You may also want to include these in your plan for future development, which you can find in the concluding chapter.

You may find it helpful to discuss the specific roles and responsibilities that sit within your current role with your manager. They may also have a view on how, overall, the work that you do can contribute to engagement and the employee experience. These roles and responsibilities may be expressly related to engagement, such as responsibility for some of those items listed above, or they may be related to broader HR work, such as where the employee lifecycle influences how people feel about the work that they do and the organization that they work for.

Supporting engagement through the employment lifecycle

Employment lifecycle: A term that describes the different stages that an employee goes through during their entire employment journey with a particular employer, from their recruitment through to leaving their role.

While many of the aspects of the lifecycle appear administrative or transactional, added together, they form a crucial part of the employee experience of work. If these processes are ineffective, inaccurate, don't take place on time or are unnecessarily bureaucratic, it is bad for the employee experience, can create stress, and can cause reputational damage to the organization and HR. Imagine, for a moment, that your organization regularly pays you incorrectly or that you had an awful induction experience which didn't give you what you need to do your job properly. It would be hard for HR or your manager to properly engage you to give your best or put effort into your work. You might also feel pretty stressed.

Each stage of the employee lifecycle can influence employee engagement. HR is responsible for many aspects of the lifecycle while others sit with people managers. We explore this further in Chapter 8.

RECRUITMENT

Recruitment processes represent an employee's first contact with the organization and, as such, they can set a tone for the longer-term employment relationship. How someone is treated during recruitment can influence whether they choose to accept a role or not. Positive experiences during recruitment can begin the journey of engagement. The stage between the offer of employment and starting (induction) can be similarly influential, helping an employee to feel welcome and ready to start work. HR can influence the experience of recruitment through efficient and effective application and hiring processes, timely communication and the provision of relevant information to candidates.

INDUCTION

Also referred to as onboarding by some organizations, induction is another crucial stage in setting the tone for the employment relationship and establishing a psychological contract. A well-structured induction process can begin to generate engagement by fostering a sense of belonging, providing clarity on roles and expectations, and integrating new employees into the team effectively. HR can influence the induction experience by ensuring that new employees are promptly provided with all the information that they need to undertake their job effectively, facilitating opportunities to build connections with colleagues, and providing comprehensive introductions to the organization and its culture, processes, history and policies.

LEARNING AND DEVELOPMENT

The ability to grow and develop is a fundamental psychological need. When employees are provided with opportunities to acquire new skills, advance their careers and achieve their goals, they are more likely to feel valued and connected to the organization. HR can influence the learning and development experience by providing comprehensive opportunities to learn and grow, including training courses, coaching and mentoring, as well as ensuring that learning and development are aligned with broader performance management activities.

REWARD AND RECOGNITION

Reward and recognition are different things. Usually, reward refers to the financial elements of an employee's terms and conditions, such as pay or bonuses. Recognition is usually non-monetary and instead is about the acknowledgement of achievement or effort. This can take many forms, from a simple thank you to a formal recognition scheme. Reward and recognition can both be powerful drivers of employee engagement (and motivation) as they can help to meet some of our basic psychological needs. HR professionals can influence the experience of reward and recognition by offering a comprehensive reward strategy and benefits, aligned where appropriate to organizational culture and objectives, and providing opportunities for employees to be recognized for the work that they do.

PERFORMANCE MANAGEMENT

Although the term 'performance management' sometimes has negative connotations associated with the management of underperformance, it actually has a much broader meaning. It encompasses how an organization (and its managers) supports people to develop, including objectives, feedback, career conversations and learning and development. Well-delivered performance management contributes to employee engagement by providing employees with a sense of purpose, goals (which can be motivational) and the ability to grow and develop as individuals. HR professionals can influence the experience of performance management by establishing fair, transparent and effective methods for managing and supporting performance, including how underperformance is fairly managed.

EXIT

Even during the exit stage, engagement can be upheld through positive experiences, such as meaningful exit interviews, recognition of contributions and efforts to maintain connections through alumni networks. HR professionals can influence the experience of leaving the organization by ensuring effective and timely processes and facilitating methods for keeping in touch with leavers.

EXERCISE

Consider how your organization addresses each stage of the employment lifecycle. Use the questions to help you, and look for potential opportunities for future improvements.
Recruitment:

- How does your organization ensure a positive candidate experience during recruitment? Is the process of joining your organization an engaging and interesting one?

- Are there any gaps in communication or processes that could be improved?

- Does your advertising, branding and recruitment process make it clear why someone would want to work for you?

- Consider your own recruitment experience when you joined the organization – did it engage you?

Induction/onboarding:

- Do you have a structured induction or onboarding process? Have you assessed its effectiveness and asked employees if it provides everything they need?
- Does it help new employees feel welcome, understand their roles and integrate into the team?
- Does the induction period include setting objectives and providing feedback?
- Do you monitor how many employees are successful during their induction period?

Learning and development:

- What opportunities does your organization provide for employees to grow, develop and progress?
- How satisfied are your employees with their opportunities to learn and develop themselves?
- Is learning and development joined up with other aspects of the employment lifecycle?

Reward and recognition:

- Does your organization offer timely reward and recognition? Are these the forms of reward and recognition that your employees value?
- How frequently and consistently are employees acknowledged for their achievements and efforts?
- Are there any aspects of how you reward and recognize people that could unintentionally demotivate or disengage people?

Performance management:

- How is performance feedback provided to employees, and how frequently?
- Are employees provided with objectives that will help them to stretch and grow?
- How effective are your performance management processes?

Exit:

- What processes are in place to ensure positive exit experiences?
- Are departing employees' contributions recognized?
- Are reasons for leaving assessed and acted upon?
- Do you keep in touch with former employees?

Can you identify any areas for improvement at any stage of the lifecycle that could positively influence the employee experience? Share your ideas and suggestions with your manager if you think it is appropriate.

STOP AND THINK

Consider your role in employee engagement at your organization.

- As an early career HR professional, how can you influence or support engagement initiatives in your organization?
- What specific actions can you take to ensure engagement drivers are embedded into everyday practices?
- How might you use your understanding of engagement to advocate for change or improvements within your organization?
- In the Conclusion, you'll find a skills assessment and action planning tool. Use this to help you reflect further on developing your skills in and knowledge of employee engagement.

Supporting employee wellbeing in practice

HR professionals may play several roles relating to employee health and wellbeing. Depending on the organization and the role itself, these could include some of the following:

- Advising managers on managing absence from work, including guidance on policy and relevant legal requirements, or planning return to work support for employees who have been absent.
- Working with occupational health providers or other specialists to identify employee support needs, especially relating to workplace adjustments or long-term health conditions.
- Managing wellbeing-related suppliers, such as EAP providers, occupational health or training providers.
- Running wellbeing events to raise awareness of health or wellbeing activities and opportunities provided by the employer.
- Delivering training for people managers on issues like absence, mental health or their role in employee health and wellbeing.
- Acting as a point of contact for employees experiencing health challenges and connecting them to appropriate resources.
- Monitoring and analysing workplace health data (such as absence or survey data) to identify trends and develop proactive solutions.
- Developing policies that relate to employee health and wellbeing, including those relating to absence or attendance.

STOP AND THINK

- What are your responsibilities concerning health and wellbeing within your specific role?
- As an early career HR professional, how can you influence or support employee health and wellbeing in your organization?
- Consider the employee lifecycle again, which we discussed earlier. Can you spot any potential stressors that can be removed or reduced during the different stages?
- How might you use your understanding of employee wellbeing to suggest improvements or make recommendations within your organization?

- Consider one action that you could personally take in your current role to enhance employee health and wellbeing. Who would you need to agree this with?

Supporting unwell employees

So far, we have discussed how to support employees to improve their wellbeing. However, the role of the HR professional will also inevitably involve working with employees experiencing ill health. This might be a temporary issue, or it might be that an individual has a long-term health condition or disability requiring ongoing support or adjustments. Ill health may or may not be related to the work that someone undertakes. Supporting employees experiencing health issues is a tertiary intervention – such interventions may need to be tailored to take into account the work, the nature of the health condition and the individual's specific needs.

Providing support will help to reduce absence rates, retain talented employees and help employee engagement.

Disability: In the UK, a disability is defined by the Equality Act 2010 as a long-term health condition that has an adverse impact on day-to-day activities.

TIP

Some countries have legislation regarding disability at work, placing legal obligations on employers to provide support or adjustments. Ensure that you understand any relevant laws that you are required to follow in addition to the guidance provided in this book.

When supporting an employee who is unwell or who has a long-term health condition, HR professionals should consider some of the following:

- Where appropriate, take advice from a medical professional on the specific circumstances. This might be from the employee's doctor or a specialist occupational health organization.
- Ask the employee what they need. Work with the individual's manager to ensure regular dialogue, and if adjustments or support are provided, check in to see if these are working as intended.
- If an employee is away from work due to their health, keep in touch. A balance is required as too much contact may not be helpful – ideally, talk to the employee about the best way to keep in touch and how often to do so.
- Support the return to work. When an employee has been away from work due to their health, returning to work can be a source of worry. Talk to them about how they can be supported to make an effective return. We discuss this further in Chapter 8.
- Check specialist guidance relating to the condition. Organizations (including charities) focused on supporting people with specific health conditions often produce guidance and information about working with the condition. These can be helpful for the employee, their manager and HR.
- Ask the employee what, if anything, they want shared with their colleagues, especially if they are away from work. This should always be the employee's choice. Remember that medical information is likely to be protected information under data protection laws.

WORKPLACE ADJUSTMENTS

Employees with health conditions may need workplace adjustments to support them in the workplace. These might be temporary, for example, to help someone make a return to work after a period of ill health, or longer-term in nature. Adjustments can help employees to make a successful return to work, support ongoing health and retain talent. Example workplace adjustments could include:

- a change in hours or work location
- amended duties
- provision of equipment
- a phased return to work (when an employee works fewer hours initially building up to their normal working pattern)
- changes to the physical working environment

Workplace adjustments should be documented, and if they are short-term, a review date set.

Occasionally, even if an organization can offer support or adjustments, an employee's health condition may mean that they are no longer able to work. In such circumstances, the organization should follow any relevant internal policies and domestic legislation.

TIP

Some countries have specific legislation about supporting employees with specific health conditions, which can include mental health. Make sure you understand any relevant legislation that applies to your context.

CHAPTER SUMMARY

- HR activities that influence engagement and wellbeing may be strategic, practical or administrative. They may be direct or operate through people managers.
- The specific activities that HR professionals undertake in relation to engagement and wellbeing vary between organizations and may depend on resources, budgets and broader organizational objectives.

- People managers are one of your key stakeholders, and without their buy-in, initiatives may fail. Be sure to manage your boundaries and work to build effective relationships based on collaboration, trust and respect.

- There can be a mismatch between the expectations of the organization and those of employees. It's important to address any unrealistic expectations about your role and responsibilities and be clear about what you can and cannot offer.

- The employee lifecycle influences employee engagement. HR professionals should consider the impact of their policies and processes during these important interactions with employees.

- Supporting employee wellbeing is a varied role and may involve working with outside providers, for example in occupational health, to identify and support employee health needs. Working closely with managers is crucial to ensure employees receive the best ongoing support.

REVIEW QUESTIONS

1   Name the different stages of the employment lifecycle.

2   List three ways that early career HR professionals can support employee engagement in practice.

3   List three ways that early career HR professionals can support employee wellbeing in practice.

Further reading

Templeman, G (2021) *The HR Business Partner Handbook: A practical guide to being your organization's strategic people expert*, Kogan Page

Price, J (2024) *The Power of HR: How to make an organizational impact as a people professional*, Kogan Page

CHAPTER EIGHT

The manager's role in engagement and wellbeing

Introduction

Following on from our discussions in Chapter 7 about the role of HR professionals in engagement and wellbeing, this chapter turns to the critical role that managers play. They can, through their day-to-day management activity, either support or damage employee wellbeing, as well as drive or detract from engagement. The manager has a significant impact on the employee experience, from when an employee joins the organization to when they leave.

We begin with a discussion on the role of good people management in engagement and wellbeing, and the skills that managers need. We look at how HR professionals can support managers to be effective in their roles and responsibilities, from providing practical day-to-day advice to assisting them with longer-term development opportunities and reflection on skills. We will also consider some tricky and sensitive issues, from helping managers support employees experiencing poor mental health to gaining buy-in for engagement and wellbeing initiatives.

LEARNING OBJECTIVES

By the end of this chapter, you will be able to:

- Describe the importance of the manager's role in employee engagement and wellbeing.

- Explain to people managers how they might support employee engagement and wellbeing.

- Summarize how HR professionals can support managers in building relevant skills to enable engagement and wellbeing, including through training programmes.

- Understand how to persuade reluctant managers to buy into employee engagement and wellbeing.

- Identify common challenges experienced by managers and explain how HR can support them with these.

- Help managers reflect on their management style and identify their own development needs.

People management for engagement and wellbeing

'Managers' can include many different people with varying duties and levels of responsibility. The size and complexity of the organization, as well as the specific managerial role, influence these individuals' responsibilities concerning wellbeing and engagement.

Senior managers typically have more responsibility with potential involvement in the strategic aspects of engagement and wellbeing. More junior managers, such as team leaders or first-line management, may have more practical responsibilities. Both have an important influence on the individuals who work for them.

The way that managers approach their day-to-day responsibilities can help engage (or disengage!) employees, although they may not necessarily be conscious of it. Everything counts, from their communication style to their behaviour and how they undertake specific people management aspects of their role, such as appraisals or supporting a new staff member. The same is true for employee health and wellbeing, which is also heavily influenced by the role and skills of people managers. Research suggests that management competencies and behaviours are the fundamental building blocks for enabling both high employee engagement and good employee health and wellbeing.[1]

In the next sections of this chapter, we consider the specific role of people managers concerning employee wellbeing and employee engagement. These two subjects both involve a need for broad people management skills and supporting behaviours.

Skills for good people management

Many of the general skills for holistic good people management also help to ensure that employees feel engaged and able to work in healthy teams and working environments. Skilled managers are:

- good communicators
- aware of their impact
- effective at providing feedback
- supportive of employee learning and development
- fair, consistent and inclusive
- good listeners, empathic and approachable
- good relationship builders
- proactive at managing issues and addressing problems

HR professionals play a key role in developing people managers at all levels of the organization. Skilled managers can enable engagement and wellbeing without even interacting with specific initiatives or activities. Later in the chapter, we discuss training that might support managers in developing employee engagement and wellbeing.

The manager's role in employee engagement

The manager's role in employee engagement is a broad one. As we've said, almost everything managers do in the workplace may influence engagement and the wider employee experience – either positively or negatively. Managers can influence employee engagement in many ways, including the following examples:

- Their involvement in the different stages of the employee lifecycle, such as recruiting, supporting new starters, managing performance and providing opportunities for learning and development.
- Their behaviour, including how they interact with people, communicate, how available they are and their general demeanour. For example, are they approachable and a good listener, and do they seem to care about their employees generally?
- How they support team dynamics, including building relationships, promoting teamwork or addressing conflict.
- How they manage workload and tasks and ensure that workloads are reasonable and manageable.
- How they recognize employees for their efforts.
- How they manage people administration, for example, responding to holiday requests, dealing with someone's pay query or answering questions on family leave. These may seem like small tasks, but they are often critically important to employees.

Managers may not be aware of just how crucial their role in employee engagement is, which can provide an opportunity for HR. This is important, as managers not only have the power to engage employees, but poor managers can demotivate, disengage and reduce health and wellbeing.

Practical ways for managers to support engagement

Here are just a few suggestions that HR professionals can make to people managers or incorporate into training and development on engagement.

- Use existing and available reward and recognition approaches. For example, is there an employee of the month (or similar) scheme or any opportunities to recognize achievement or hard work? Celebrate small wins.
- Create opportunities for social connection and relationships. Organize a team lunch or an activity, a volunteer day or even a friendly team challenge. Participation should always be optional!
- Encourage your team to undertake learning and development. Share internal opportunities and proactively suggest training or development that you think might suit specific team members.
- Have regular one-to-one meetings or check-ins with your team. Many organization-wide policies require managers to have at least annual performance reviews – but these should be an absolute minimum. Scheduled one-to-one meetings with team members provide time to discuss concerns and review progress. They also help to build a strong relationship.
- Share your availability or schedule time every week when your team know you will be available for casual chats, questions or anything they need to raise. This could be in-person or online.

These ideas can be incorporated with the practical suggestions for employee wellbeing, which are set out later in the chapter. Remember, engagement and wellbeing are often interconnected and influenced by the same type of activities, manager behaviour and organizational culture.

WHAT WOULD YOU DO?
Number 8

Your organization-wide employee engagement survey indicates that one department has significantly lower levels of job satisfaction and higher levels of stress than the rest of the organization. You receive some informal feedback that one manager in the department is difficult to work with and is setting unrealistic targets.

- How could you further investigate the results of the employee survey?
- How would you approach the manager to discuss this issue?
- What immediate actions could you take?

You may find it helpful to revisit Chapter 3 when considering your response.

The manager's role in employee wellbeing

The manager's role in employee wellbeing has two distinct elements:

- Practical activities, such as supporting employees who are experiencing ill-health or engaging with services like occupational health.
- Creating a culture for employee wellbeing through behaviour and management style.

Each of these elements incorporates different roles and responsibilities. The first element, practical activities, often involve tertiary wellbeing interventions (discussed in Chapter 6). They are sometimes accompanied by relevant HR policies and processes, such as absence or attendance policies, that set out how such issues are managed by the organization. These policies and processes may be based on relevant employment laws and, therefore, should always be followed carefully. Helping managers understand these requirements and how to stay legally compliant is a key role for HR professionals.

The second element, focused on culture, requires a broader skill set, including some of the topics listed in the previous section. HR professionals can help managers here, too, by providing relevant learning and development opportunities. While managers cannot necessarily influence the culture of the whole organization, they can influence the culture within their teams. Through day-to-day actions, they can send a clear signal about the importance of wellbeing and help create a culture where wellbeing is discussed and prioritized.

Practical ways for managers to support wellbeing

Within their day-to-day activities, people managers can take many actions to support health and wellbeing within their teams. Here are a few suggestions that HR professionals may wish to make:

- Wellbeing check-ins – managers should be encouraged to check in regularly with employees about their wellbeing. This could be done informally or form part of other management conversations, such as one-to-ones or objectives catch-ups.
- Promote flexible working arrangements – these can help employees to achieve a good work-life balance.
- Manage workloads effectively – ensure that no team member is overloaded.
- Use resources and interventions – encourage the use of wellbeing resources and interventions provided by the organization.
- Be a good role model for healthy working practices – this will be visible to teams and encourage them to adopt similar practices.
- Talking about wellbeing in teams – talking about wellbeing can help to normalize the conversation.

- Recognize and celebrate achievements – acknowledging employees' accomplishments can boost morale and reinforce a positive work environment (also supporting engagement).
- Promote regular breaks – encourage employees to step away from work to recharge and avoid burnout.
- Look out for signs of poor wellbeing or work-life balance – have proactive conversations with employees if they identify any potential areas for concern.

Managers should also be encouraged to take opportunities to learn about health and wellbeing at work and their specific role; we will discuss this later in this chapter.

Managers supporting mental health at work

Poor managers can contribute to employees' stress levels and negatively impact their mental health. The CIPD suggests that people managers have three key roles to play in supporting mental health at work:[2]

1   Prevention (helping people to stay well).
2   Early intervention (spotting the signs that someone might be experiencing poor mental health).
3   Support (which may include general assistance throughout the employment lifecycle, but, more specifically, helping people to return to work if they have been absent due to poor mental health).

In addition to some of the suggestions in the previous section, HR can help managers to support employee mental health through the following.

WELLNESS ACTION PLANS

The mental health charity Mind highlights the benefits of Wellness Action Plans.[3] These are personalized plans, documenting discussions about what can keep an employee mentally healthy at work. They can be especially useful if an employee has been experiencing poor mental health or has taken absence from work for a mental health condition.

SUPPORTING RETURN TO WORK

If an employee has taken mental health-related absence from work, returning to work can be daunting. When the return to work is supported by their immediate manager, employees are more likely to have an effective and sustained return. Assisted by HR where appropriate, managers should be encouraged to have an open and confidential conversation with the employee, ideally in advance of their return date. This conversation can encompass discussions about needs, concerns and adjustments that may be required and can culminate in a personalized return to work plan. Regular check-ins to monitor progress and amend the plan as necessary will all help to successfully re-integrate employees. As we discuss later in the chapter, HR can equip managers to spot the signs of poor mental health and have helpful and constructive wellbeing conversations.

STOP AND THINK

Consider the managers you work with and the three roles that the CIPD suggest managers should play in supporting mental health. How competent are your managers in:

- helping people to stay well (prevention)?
- spotting the signs that someone is not well (early intervention)?
- providing support for maintaining good mental health?

Does your organization provide any formal training or guidance in any of these areas? Can you identify any gaps in learning, skills or behaviours? If so, how could you help address these development needs? Consider different options and how you can make a difference.

Training managers on engagement and wellbeing

Equipping managers with the skills, knowledge and behaviour to enable employee engagement and wellbeing helps them become better managers overall, support employee health and wellbeing (including mental health) and drive employee engagement. This is not only beneficial to employees but to the organization as a whole – better engagement and wellbeing drive positive organizational outcomes. HR professionals are well-placed to help managers develop these critical leadership skills.

Effective training programs should begin by helping managers understand the fundamental concepts of engagement and wellbeing and how these factors influence employees and organizational success. Relevant subjects should include some of those topics discussed in this book, such as the drivers and detractors of engagement and wellbeing, barriers to achieving them, techniques for improvement and relevant evidence. As we have explored, these subjects are interconnected and mutually supporting; when managers gain the relevant skills and knowledge and put them into practice, they can create a working environment where employees feel motivated, valued and supported.

HR professionals are often the organizational custodians of wellbeing and engagement policies, strategies and approaches, but managers deliver the policies on a day-to-day basis (sometimes with HR support).

On a practical level, manager training on wellbeing and engagement should include some of the following, tailored to the level of manager:

· Relevant foundational theories and research, presented in an accessible way, tailored to the management level.
· Insights into the impact of their leadership style on team wellbeing and engagement.

- Practical strategies for enabling engagement and wellbeing within the managerial role.
- Skills for putting these strategies into practice.

Common techniques for management development include formal training courses, action learning (giving people a real-life situation to tackle in groups), coaching or mentoring. There is no 'right' way to provide learning and development to people managers. Budget, resources and time all need to be considered. Similarly, there is no simple list of what should be covered in training and development within these two topic areas. Some suggestions for relevant topics are below; use this as a guide, but adapt them as necessary to suit your context.

Before determining what to include in any training course or development activity, you need to understand the current level of skills and behaviours amongst existing managers. The boxed exercise can help with this.

EXERCISE

Reflect on managers at your organization and their skills, knowledge and behaviour.

- What formal management development is (or has been) provided to people managers, and how is (or was) employee engagement and wellbeing addressed?

- How effectively do managers implement the different aspects of the employee lifecycle, discussed in the previous chapter? Are they undertaken promptly, following policy and good practice?

- To what extent do you think your organization's managers understand the concepts of employee engagement and wellbeing? Give evidence for your answer.

- Do you believe that managers understand the potential impact of their day-to-day behaviour, style and activity on engagement and wellbeing? What evidence can you give to back up your answer and where do you see areas for improvement?

- How do the answers to these questions differ depending on the 'level' of managers in the organization?

- Are there any barriers preventing managers in your organization from effectively supporting employee engagement and wellbeing?

Use the answers to these questions, along with the suggestions for formal training later in this chapter, and key learnings from Chapter 6, to consider how you can help managers develop the skills and behaviours they need to effectively support engagement and wellbeing. Consider one action that you could take and discuss this with your manager.

Training on employee health and wellbeing

Managers may benefit from learning about some of the following topics on employee health and wellbeing:

- Organizational policies on attendance or absence and an overview of any relevant legal responsibilities or requirements.
- Common mental health conditions and early warning signs and symptoms.
- The causes of stress and mental health in the workplace – and how they can be reduced or addressed.
- How to have a wellbeing conversation or create a wellbeing action plan.
- The link between management styles and behaviours and employee wellbeing – how they might personally influence an employee's health, wellbeing and stress levels.
- Common wellbeing interventions and how they can help managers and employees.
- Supporting attendance, such as through reasonable adjustments for employees who have health conditions.

- Being a good role model for wellbeing and promoting the importance of health and wellbeing within their teams.
- The drivers and detractors of wellbeing at work and what managers can personally influence.

Training on employee engagement

Managers may benefit from learning about some of the following topics on employee engagement:

- Theoretical insights into the drivers and detractors of employee engagement – what helps to motivate people and engage them with their work and the organization.
- The benefits of engaged employees and how this can contribute to business and team outcomes (and their own goals and objectives as a people manager). This can be accompanied by insights into the potential business issues that can arise from employees who are not engaged.
- How employee engagement and wellbeing are linked and mutually supporting.
- The role of people managers in employee engagement and how they can influence engagement both positively and negatively through their day-to-day activity and behaviour.
- How the activities that they undertake in the employment lifecycle, such as how they recruit, support new starters or undertake performance management, will influence the employee experience and broader employee engagement.
- How to recognize and respond to the different ways that team members need to be motivated.
- The importance of reward and recognition for engagement and motivation. How to reward and recognize employees in line with existing organization policies or approaches.
- How to identify signs that an employee may be disengaged, demotivated or dissatisfied, and how to address these signs.

Getting buy-in from managers

As we've said, not every manager recognizes the importance of their role in employee health and wellbeing. They may see it as an HR or occupational health responsibility, or they may not feel confident about how to get involved. This can be especially true if there are tricky issues like mental health or long-term health conditions to consider.

Occasionally, managers may not agree with HR advice or recommendations on matters related to employee engagement and wellbeing. There can be a range of reasons for this. They may be unpersuaded by the evidence or business case – subjects we have discussed previously. They may feel that advice or activities are too expensive, time consuming or unaligned with their objectives. Many managers are time poor and may not feel that they have the time to give to engagement and wellbeing. They may prefer their own solutions for dealing with their HR challenges, or they might just want HR to do this work for them, a subject we also touched on in Chapter 7 when we discussed boundaries.

This can be a tricky area to navigate, especially for the early career HR professional. Chapter 7 sets out how to gain buy-in if you want to start new projects or initiatives. Below are a few tips on working with, and persuading, reluctant managers to act:

- Recognize their challenges. Show managers that you understand the issues they face and highlight how you can support them through HR activities. For example, working with them to support employees back to work from absence or helping them to recruit can alleviate workload pressures.
- Understand their part of the business. You will be the most effective partner if you have a strong understanding of their part of the organization and how it functions.

- Work continuously on your relationships. Relationships are key; when relationships are strong and managers recognize your expertise and knowledge, they will be more likely to accept advice and work with you.
- Be clear about the benefits. Ensure the manager knows the reasons behind your recommendations and the benefits of following your approach. For example, are you trying to minimize their legal risk, or is there a policy they need to follow?
- Tailor your approach to different managers. For example, some managers might want to see data to back up your recommendations, while others won't. Adjust your approach to what will resonate best with each manager.

TIP

Where possible, avoid simply telling managers that they need to follow a policy. While this might be true, it is not necessarily a way to get strong commitment and may cause resentment if the manager feels that this is not right for them or their operational needs. If there are good reasons for the policy, such as managing legal risk or meeting an organization-wide commitment, make sure that you explain this clearly.

Manager challenges – and how HR can help

In Chapter 7, we talked about the importance of HR professionals and managers having an effective working relationship, and HR having a good understanding of the role of the manager and their priorities. All managers have their challenges from time to time. These might be operational or relate to the general people management aspects of their role. This section considers some of these challenges and the role that HR professionals can play in helping managers address them. While some of these challenges are not specific to employee engagement and wellbeing, left unaddressed they might have a negative influence on the employee experience, culture and how employees feel about work. As we have already seen, helping managers to get better at this aspect of their jobs can only be good for the employees who work for them.

Transitioning to management

New or first-time managers can find their new role challenging for several reasons. There are new policies and processes to learn, a team to get to know and probably new objectives to deliver against. Challenges can be compounded if the manager has been promoted within their team and is now line-managing former colleagues. This might be the first time that a manager has been responsible for employee engagement and wellbeing – as well as all the other activities of the employment lifecycle. HR can help new managers by guiding them on policies and processes, signposting them to training and development, and acting as a coach and advisor. Setting up regular meetings initially can help them settle confidently into their role and build a trusted relationship.

Understanding legal and policy requirements

HR professionals often have a good knowledge of employment law or internal policies as they use them regularly. This is not necessarily true of all managers. Sometimes, policies or legal requirements are difficult to understand, or their requirements might not align with how a manager would like to approach a situation. HR professionals can help managers by providing concise explanations (as managers may also be busy) and advice tailored to the circumstances. When managers cannot take their preferred course of action, explain why and where appropriate signpost them to relevant sources of information (if they would find this helpful).

Having difficult or sensitive conversations

People managers may find themselves having a range of difficult conversations. These could range from discussing a sensitive health issue, providing feedback about underperformance or even dealing with a dismissal. Not all managers will have experience in these situations, but even if they do, they may still find them difficult and stressful. HR professionals can support managers in such situations by providing guidance on what to say and talking through potential employee responses and how to handle these. Some managers might even benefit from role-playing the conversation with their HR partner or having them present in the room. It is always a good idea to ask a manager what kind of help they need from you, rather than make assumptions.

Managing team conflict

Conflict at work can arise for lots of reasons. Employees may have a personality clash, different work styles, competing priorities or simply have a misunderstanding. Conflict is damaging to teams. It can also harm engagement and culture and be a potential source of employee stress or absence. HR professionals can help managers to address conflict by providing advice and guidance on potential strategies. If they have the necessary skills, HR professionals can even facilitate conversations between team members. There may also be relevant HR policies and procedures that managers should be advised of.

When HR professionals work in partnership with managers, supporting and guiding them with tricky challenges, it benefits working relationships and credibility. From time to time, early career professionals may also find themselves supporting a manager with a tricky issue that they have themselves not dealt with previously. Always be prepared to seek advice from more experienced colleagues, and always check relevant employment law and internal policies before providing advice.

Encouraging reflection on management style

Managers have such a powerful role to play in employee engagement and wellbeing that, as well as providing training, they should be encouraged to reflect on their management style and how it influences these two important subjects. Use the exercise below to encourage managers to reflect, adapting it for your own needs if helpful. Handle these conversations carefully, as not all managers want to reflect or see that they need to. Consider the best way to approach such a suggestion; it could form part of the training we discussed previously in this chapter.

EXERCISE

Use some of these questions to help managers reflect on their management style. The questions take into account factors that we know influence engagement and wellbeing:

- How often do you have one-on-one conversations with your team members? Do these conversations include a wellbeing check-in?

- How do you recognize and celebrate the contributions and achievements of your team members?

- How well do you understand what motivates each member of your team individually?

- Do you tailor your management style to your team member? Could you say what motivates the different members of your current team?

- How do you assess whether the workload of your team is appropriate and manageable?

- Do all of your team have up-to-date, relevant objectives that are regularly reviewed?

- Do you regularly provide clear and constructive feedback? Can you think of a recent example?

- How would you know if one of your team was stressed or experiencing burnout?

- Are there any areas in your management approach that you feel need improvement? What steps are you taking to address them?

- How do you model work-life balance and wellbeing for your team?

- How do you ensure that your communication style fosters an inclusive and open environment?

- What steps do you take to build empathy and trust within your team?

- How do you encourage healthy work habits, such as taking breaks and maintaining work-life balance?

Discuss the answers to these questions and use them to guide a conversation about any learning and development the manager may wish to undertake.

CHAPTER SUMMARY

- Employee engagement and wellbeing are heavily influenced by managers and how they behave, act and implement organizational policies relating to people. This includes how they administer key elements of the employee lifecycle.

- HR professionals can help managers to develop skills to enable them to be effective in these key subject areas. HR and managers can work in partnership to mutually enable and support engagement and wellbeing.

- Engagement and wellbeing should be incorporated into management development programmes or formalized learning. The specific content of such learning should be tailored to current skill levels, budgets, resources and organizational goals.

- HR professionals may encounter push-back from managers who, for various reasons, are reluctant to buy into employee engagement and wellbeing initiatives. There are several things you can do to persuade managers to act.

- Managers can experience a range of challenges related to engagement and wellbeing, which HR professionals can support them with.

- The most effective managers reflect on their management style and are aware of any development needs to help them become a force for employee engagement and wellbeing. HR professionals can play a key supportive role in this process.

REVIEW QUESTIONS

1 List five skills managers need to successfully support employees to be engaged and well at work.

2 Identify at least one way that managers can support employees experiencing poor mental health.

3 What should be included in a manager training programme on employee wellbeing?

4 Explain how an early career HR professional can help to encourage managers to reflect on their management style.

Further reading

CIPD and Mind Charity, People managers' guide to mental health, www.mind.org.uk/media-a/4660/mental-health-at-work-1_tcm18-10567.pdf (archived at https://perma.cc/47WT-352H)

CIPD and Department of Work and Pensions, Recruiting, managing and developing disabled people: A practical guide for managers, www.gov.uk/government/publications/disability-confident-and-cipd-guide-for-line-managers-on-employing-people-with-a-disability-or-health-condition/guide-for-line-managers-recruiting-managing-and-developing-people-with-a-disability-or-health-condition (archived at https://perma.cc/3YFN-LEER)

Endnotes

1 www.cipd.org/globalassets/media/knowledge/knowledge-hub/reports/ full-report18364.pdf (archived at https://perma.cc/6BEC-Q4GW)
2 www.cipd.org/uk/knowledge/guides/mental-health-support-guide/ (archived at https://perma.cc/A68E-GKVK)
3 www.mind.org.uk/media/lbahso3x/mind-wellness-action-plan-work-place.pdf (archived at https://perma.cc/RX67-AVVC)

Conclusion

This book has sought to introduce employee engagement and wellbeing to the early career HR professional. This concluding chapter provides further guidance on developing your skills, knowledge, competencies and behaviours to support your future in these two crucial areas of HR work.

Reflect on your current skills as you work through the chapter, keeping in mind your organization's culture and desired future career direction.

Remember that both employee engagement and wellbeing are developing areas of HR. Although they have both been part of HR activities and strategies for some time, new research frequently emerges, and the ever-changing context of work demands that HR professionals adapt their approaches in line with changes.

> **LEARNING OBJECTIVES**
>
> By the end of this chapter, you will be able to:
>
> - Review and reflect on your skills in the areas of employee engagement and wellbeing.
> - Identify areas for future learning.
> - Develop an action plan for continuous professional development.
> - Explain how the future of work might influence the work of HR professionals in the areas of engagement and wellbeing.

HR skills for engagement and wellbeing

HR professionals need numerous different skills to implement engagement and wellbeing initiatives, and beyond. These include technical knowledge on subjects, encompassing research evidence and relevant legislation. They must also employ what are often (but perhaps incorrectly) termed 'soft' skills, such as listening, communication, organization, problem-solving and decision-making.

The specific demands of an HR career also mean that skills in areas like conflict management, managing stakeholder expectations and handling sensitive conversations are also important. Finally, and also related to the unique work of the profession, HR practitioners must demonstrate integrity and confidentiality and take an ethical and inclusive approach to their work. The UK CIPD's profession map, which sets out core behaviours and competencies, also highlights the importance of business acumen and commercial understanding.[1] These skills ensure HR professionals' recommendations and projects are considered in the context of organizational goals and potential return on investment, rather than simply being focused on the benefit to employees.

Together, this mix of skills, behaviours and competencies helps HR professionals be trusted partners and deliver value for their organizations.

Reviewing your knowledge, skills and behaviour

The 'review questions' at the end of each chapter can help you assess your understanding of the subjects discussed throughout this book. To further help you assess your skills in employee engagement and wellbeing, you may find it useful to undertake the skills and knowledge assessment exercise in the box.

KNOWLEDGE, SKILLS AND BEHAVIOUR ASSESSMENT – EMPLOYEE ENGAGEMENT AND WELLBEING

Ask yourself the following questions.

Knowledge

- To what extent are you aware of current trends, research and good practice in workplace engagement and wellbeing?
- Can you summarize the factors, either within or outside of work, that affect employee engagement and health and wellbeing?
- Can you identify the signs and symptoms of poor mental health, disengagement or demotivation?
- Can you explain the benefits of your workplace wellbeing activities and engagement initiatives and events to employees and managers?
- Do you fully understand any policies within your organization on subjects related to engagement and wellbeing, such as attendance or absence? Can you also identify relevant employment laws in the management of employees experiencing poor health or disabilities?
- Do you understand the causes of absence or ill-health, employee turnover or disengagement within your organization?
- Do you understand how to measure the success or return on investment of a wellbeing or engagement activity or intervention?

Skills

- Can you confidently communicate the importance of engagement or wellbeing to senior leaders and secure their buy-in for initiatives or recommendations?
- How effectively can you listen to employees' or managers' concerns about engagement and wellbeing without judgment and respond appropriately?

- Can you facilitate open discussions about engagement and wellbeing within teams, ensuring a safe and supportive environment?
- Are you a good role model for wellbeing and work-life balance at work?
- Can you analyse data about wellbeing and engagement, and identify areas of concern or potential for improvement?

Behaviour

- How do you ensure you behave ethically in your HR work, especially when dealing with difficult, sensitive or confidential matters?
- How do you ensure that you continually develop as an HR professional?
- How do you ensure inclusivity and fairness in your HR work?

TIP

Below are ten top tips to help you continue your learning and development in engagement and wellbeing. Follow these to maximize your potential for future success.

1 Continue to develop your knowledge of employee engagement and wellbeing. This will help you to make good evidence-based decisions and advise your organization effectively.

2 Build your network. Learning from other HR professionals contributes to your overall career success. Attend events and build an online network, following industry experts and joining groups.

3 Look at external good practice. Keeping up to date with what other organizations are doing can help you develop new ideas. Check out case studies, talks, webinars and events.

4 Look for learning opportunities internally, such as learning from more experienced colleagues. Volunteer for projects or programmes that can support your development.

5 Take a continuous learning approach to HR subjects in general. Stay current on industry trends through online courses, podcasts, books and articles.

6 Engage outside of HR. Learning about your organization and its managers will help you to provide high-quality advice about engagement and wellbeing aligned with their needs.

7 Seek a mentor. If you have a particular interest in employee engagement or wellbeing, seek out a more senior professional from whom you can learn more.

8 Get familiar with your organizational data on wellbeing and engagement to offer effective advice and recommendations.

9 Take opportunities to build relationships with senior leaders in your organization to position yourself as a trusted advisor, advancing your HR career and increasing your influence.

10 Take time to understand your organization's mission, values and objectives. Consider how employee engagement and wellbeing activities can help support those goals.

Mental health in the HR profession

Working in the HR profession can involve stressors that are not necessarily present in other roles or functions. We may have to manage difficult and sensitive situations, from complaints about harassment or bullying to managing redundancy situations. We may need to support employees going through difficult times, such as health problems or bereavement. Work of this nature can be stressful or draining, especially for early career professionals navigating these situations for the first time.

In addition, it can be difficult for HR professionals to engage in wellbeing activities available to other employees. For example, if the HR department offers support for stress during a time of organizational change, those HR professionals involved might not feel able to access that support themselves.

It is important, therefore, for HR professionals to take care of their wellbeing at work and to be particularly mindful of the impact their work might have on their mental health. This should be considered a skill in its own right.

Self-care is important, as is seeking support from colleagues or managers. Taking breaks, switching off from work and engaging in activities that enable wellbeing, either inside or outside of work, all help HR professionals to stay well and remain resilient – as well as reduce the risk of stress or burnout. Where available, HR should also engage with relevant support services if they need them, such as an Employee Assistance Programme.

STOP AND THINK

Consider the type of HR work that you do, or that you are seeking.

- What potential stressors can you identify that might exist within the role?
- Consider how you can maintain your health and wellbeing while undertaking your work.
- Identify specific steps and activities that you can take.

The future of employee engagement and wellbeing

The future of work is a hot topic. As long as there have been management thinkers, writers and researchers, there have been attempts to predict how work is going to change in the near- and long-term future. Some of these predictions have come true, whereas others have been less accurate. Ways of working are often disrupted by changing economic, political, social or technological forces, or just changes in what customers want. At the same time, some aspects of work are stubborn and hard to shift.

For example, predictions that remote work would soon be a dominant way of working were made in the late 1970s and early 1980s but did not become even close to realized until a global pandemic.

This presents a challenge for the HR professional. While we cannot accurately predict the future of work, we can make some assumptions about it. It is highly likely, for example, that work and workplaces will continue to see change driven by technology in the years to come, with increasing digitalization and the use of AI. The HR professional, therefore, needs to be grounded in the present while also scanning the horizon, looking for possible changes that might affect their organization and what this would, in turn, mean for the people who work for it and how they need to be hired, supported, engaged, managed, trained and rewarded. This will allow HR as a function to add value and impact through the work that they do, further cementing them as trusted advisors. Here are a few tips for early career HR professionals who want to future-proof themselves and their career:

- Stay informed about emerging trends in technology, such as AI, automation and digital transformation. Look out for news items, reports from think tanks or consultancies, or read thought pieces.
- Identify key thinkers and writers about the future of work and follow them on their social media feeds.
- Search for organizations who research and write about the future of work and sign up for their updates and new information.
- Look out for content specific to your own industry and how it might evolve in the future.

Where you can, even if you don't have all the answers or potential solutions, share the insights you have learned with your team or managers in your organization. This can help kick start thinking and discussion and raise your profile.

Action planning for continuous professional development

This book has offered opportunities to reflect on your current role and practice, as well as recommendations for practice and practical tips and exercises to cement your learning. The final step is to reflect on what you have read, think about your own career goals and ambitions in accordance with your current skills, knowledge and experience, and combine these into a plan for your continuing professional development (CPD).

CPD is a process through which you plan for your future learning and development to develop your professional HR practice, considering your current experiences, skills, knowledge and behaviour. Everyone's plan will be different, reflecting their unique situation, experiences to date, opportunities and goals. Here, we focus on how to build your skills in employee engagement and wellbeing, but you should consider your HR practice more widely, too. No HR topic is truly independent of another, and as this book has demonstrated, the different elements of HR work align, interconnect and overlap. When HR work is done well at both strategic and operational levels, each element of people practice mutually supports the employee experience.

HR professional SWOT analysis

You may have heard of a SWOT analysis or undertaken one during your academic studies. A personal SWOT analysis is a valuable tool for early-career HR professionals to reflect on their strengths, weaknesses, opportunities and threats concerning their skills, experience, capabilities and knowledge. It can help you to reflect, identifying what you are already good at, as well as areas that need further development to progress your career as an HR professional. In the next section, we look at translating the personal SWOT analysis into a plan – this can include not just working on your development areas but maximizing existing areas of strength.

The SWOT analysis process is simple:

1   List your strengths. What skills, knowledge and experience do you have concerning employee engagement and wellbeing?

2   Reflect on your weaknesses or areas for development concerning engagement and wellbeing. These might include areas where you have less practical experience or theoretical knowledge, where you have less confidence or where you feel that you can learn more.

3   What opportunities are available to you? Think about ideas from the section on the future of work or opportunities more specific to your organization or role. Consider workplace trends, opportunities for informal learning and formal training or any other chances that might exist (or that you can create!) to further advance your skills, experience and knowledge.

4   Consider potential threats. These might be external factors, such as changes in the political, social, technological or economic landscape. They might be internal (within your organization) or personal (such as a particular trait that you are aware of). Try to think of anything that might get in the way of you developing your competency in the fields of engagement and wellbeing.

After you have completed the exercise, use your reflections and ideas to create an action plan. Think about how you might tackle development areas and how to ensure that potential threats do not derail your future professional development.

Action plan

Creating an action plan for continuous learning can help to provide structure and clarity to your learning and personal development. It can help you identify goals, set timelines and break down what you want to learn and how you want to

TABLE 9.1 An action plan for continuous learning

What is your specific objective?	How will achieving this objective support your HR career or ambitions?	When will you achieve this goal by?	How will you know when you have been successful?	What resources do you need to achieve your objective?
Build my personal online network of HR professionals through joining groups and connecting with industry leaders.	Expose me to new ideas and the HR activities of other organizations. Potentially generate new ideas for my own role.	The end of the calendar year initially – but continue on an ongoing basis.	My network will be rich and diverse and I will have a minimum of 500 professional connections.	Access to LinkedIn. Time to dedicate to searching for and connecting with relevant contacts.
Review my organization's engagement survey data from previous surveys.	I will build a knowledge of employee preferences, concerns, suggestions and perspectives. This will help me to shape my HR work accordingly.	The end of this quarter.	I will have read and understood previous survey data and can summarize this effectively.	Access to survey data.

develop into discreet, manageable steps. It also helps you to track your progress.

Using your SWOT self-assessment, any other reflection exercises you have undertaken in this book and the template provided, set yourself some learning goals. Aim for at least three objectives to further your skills, knowledge or experience. Provide as much detail as possible when drafting your action plan and the specific goals within it. Table 9.1 shows an action plan with the first two rows completed as examples.

Further reading

How HR can look after their own mental health: Guide for people professionals, CIPD, www.cipd.org/uk/knowledge/guides/hr-mental-health/ (archived at https://perma.cc/9MM8-JKEG)

Endnote

1 www.cipd.org/globalassets/media/comms/the-people-profession/profession-map-pdfs/profession-map-nov-2024.pdf (archived at https://perma.cc/QZ69-GEVN)

Answers to 'What would you do?' exercises

This appendix gives some suggested responses or approaches for the 'What would you do?' exercises included in this book. Each of these answers is based on current UK legislation, relevant codes of practice and good employment practice. They are indicative only; you may decide that in your particular organizational context, a different approach would be more suited or supportive of your wellbeing and engagement strategies.

WHAT WOULD YOU DO? NUMBER 1

Several of the academic theories discussed in the chapter could be useful to help you understand the reactions from the team. Under Job Demands-Resources theory, high workload can be a job demand that leads to stress or burnout and disengagement. Herzberg's theory tells us that pay and rewards can be dissatisfiers; the removed bonus, therefore, could be leading to levels of dissatisfaction amongst the team.

The manager could seek to address what they can, taking these theories into account. They may not, for example, be able to influence an organizational decision on bonuses, but they may be able to reduce workloads and the demands placed on employees during this time. They can also take action to motivate employees; several of the discussed theories, for example, tell us about the importance of development and personal growth in motivation and engagement. The manager could review oppor-tunities to provide development activities within the scope of the current organizational challenges.

WHAT WOULD YOU DO? NUMBER 2
Potential questions for the manager:

- What have you observed that has made you concerned the employee is disengaged? Can you give me an example?
- How is this different to their normal behaviour? What is the employee usually like when they are engaged?
- Has the employee shared any concerns or feedback with you or others?
- Can you identify a potential reason for the disengagement or change in the employee?

The manager could initiate a conversation with the employee, sharing their observations and asking questions to seek to under-stand. Conversations of this nature should be non-judgemental, and the manager needs to practice active listening throughout and show empathy. If the employee shares any relevant informa-tion or problems, the manager can engage in a more detailed conversation about how the issue can be addressed.

WHAT WOULD YOU DO? NUMBER 3
Questions you could ask the manager:

- What makes you think that engagement and motivation are low? What have you observed or what feedback have you received?
- What is different about the team now compared to previously?
- What could you do to check your thoughts about their engagement? Do you have any data sources or feedback that can help inform you?
- Have there been any recent changes or events that might influence engagement? Can you identify any potential causes from what you know?

Use the list of quick wins for ideas – are there any of these that the manager could implement to lift engagement and motivation in the team? For example, social activities, recognition or sharing information. The manager could also talk to employees, individually or as a team, to seek feedback about how they are feeling and find out if they have any suggestions for improving ways of working or dynamics. This conversation will help the manager to establish if there really is an issue and provide valuable evidence on the reasons why. This can inform a longer-term approach towards team engagement.

WHAT WOULD YOU DO? NUMBER 4

This is a complex situation; it is still important to recognize and motivate remaining staff while remaining sensitive to what is happening elsewhere in the organization. Recognition for those employees should still be made, but this should be one-to-one or low-key rather than lavish or public. It may be appropriate to make remaining employees' rewards non-monetary to ensure that the organization does not send the wrong message about costs. Recognition can also be framed around how that team's success is helping the organization to navigate a difficult time as purpose and meaning can help to drive motivation. They also need to ensure the team has manageable and achievable goals. Motivation theories, discussed earlier in the book, can also provide additional insight.

The manager of the team should lead with empathy and purpose. They will need to acknowledge the broader context in other areas of the organization; honesty and transparency are almost always the best policy. The organization can work to ensure high-quality, regular and transparent communication from leaders, recognition of achievement and contribution for team members and a fair redundancy process for employees who are leaving the organization.

WHAT WOULD YOU DO? NUMBER 5

You should seek to understand more about what is going on within appropriate boundaries – remember that you are not a mental health expert and should not give advice outside of related work matters. Some potential questions:

- Can you tell me more about how you are feeling? How long have you been feeling this way?
- Have you sought any help for the way that you are feeling?
- Is there anything work-related that is contributing to how you are feeling?
- What do you think would help to improve the situation?
- Is there any particular reason why you would not be comfortable talking to your manager?

It may also be necessary to remind the individual that there are limits to the help you can provide if they are not willing for information to be shared.

You could signpost the employee to more specialist sources of help, including wellbeing services if you have them, or encourage them to see their doctor. Acknowledge that they have sought help from you and that this is a positive step. Ask if there is any particular help that they are seeking at this time. Unless the employee has any specific concerns about telling their manager, encourage them to do so, as it may be difficult to implement support or adjustments without their involvement. It may be appropriate for you to attend such a meeting. Explore any next steps or actions following the meeting.

WHAT WOULD YOU DO? NUMBER 6

You could investigate this issue by interrogating the data further. For example, break down data by team, role type, location (if applicable) or function. Look for patterns – are certain absences higher in particular teams or roles? You could also investigate which aspects of work undertaken, or the way that work is designed, could be causing the musculoskeletal issues. This may include talking to employees, observing work or working with health and safety colleagues or representatives if you have them. Interventions to support musculoskeletal health could include ergonomic assessments, training in safe lifting, movement or carrying, encouraging desk-based workers to adopt good posture and take breaks, providing suitable furniture, or, in the case of ongoing issues, referral to occupational health or specialist services for treatment.

WHAT WOULD YOU DO? NUMBER 7

While HR plays an important role in supporting and advising managers on absence management, the day-to-day responsibility rests with the manager, as it does with all forms of performance management. There are several reasons for this that you could use to frame your response to the manager. Absence issues are often best understood in the context of the employee's role and team, something that the manager should be best placed to know. Similarly, managers are most likely to understand what adjustments or support can be provided to address the absence.

Absence does not need to be managed formally in all cases, and involving HR might indicate that this is a formal process. You can explain these reasons, and then ask how you can help them prepare for the conversations, including preparing talking points or questions, and reviewing the absence policy. Remember that reluctance to undertake such conversations might indicate that the manager feels uncertain or uncomfortable, and approaching this from a place of support and guidance may help to address these concerns. If appropriate, you could offer to attend meetings to support the manager.

WHAT WOULD YOU DO? NUMBER 8

You could dig deeper into the data by looking at the specific questions that are of concern and analysing the data against different demographics to see if there are any important trends or differences. Are all team members reporting low scores, or are they clustered around specific sub-teams or roles?

It would also be useful to establish if this is a new trend or whether this department has previously had lower scores in previous surveys. You will need to consider whether or not the manager in question is contributing to the lower scores; at the same time, you should remain open-minded to other factors within this team contributing to the differences.

It is a good idea to talk to all managers about their engagement survey scores if possible; have an open conversation with the manager about their scores and any reasons that they can identify that might contribute to the lower score. If appropriate, you may also want to involve their manager, approaching this from the position of seeking to understand more and improve employee perceptions. Depending on the circumstances, you may also consider holding a focus group or feedback session with employees in the area to discuss scores and how to improve ways of working.

Looking for another book?

Explore our award-winning
books from global business
experts in Human Resources,
Learning and Development

Scan the code to browse

www.koganpage.com/hr-learning-
development

Our Brand New HR Skills Series

All the knowledge and skills for your HR Career